PERCEPTIVE BOWLING

PERCEPTIVE BOWLING

A TEXT FOR THE
SERIOUS BOWLER

Robert Strickland

Robert H. Strickland Associates, Everett, WA 98206-1388

Cover and book design: Walter R. Haessner
Cover photo: Chuck Rogers, Atlanta, GA
Typesetting: Maria L. Montijo

ISBN 10: 0963591916 / ISBN 13: 9780963591913
Library of Congress Catalog Card No. 80-54249

Copyright 1980 by Robert Strickland

All rights reserved. No part of this book may be reproduced or transmitted in any form or by any means, electronic or mechanical, including photocopying, recording or by any information storage or retrieval system, without permission in writing from the publisher

Second Printing 1983
Third Printing with Corrections and Annotations 2011

Printed in the United States of America

Robert H. Strickland Associates
P O Box 1388, Everett, WA 98206-1388

Contents

Preface 5
    Addendum to Preface 7

Acknowledgements 9

A Fond Remembrance 11

Introduction 13

1   **A Proper Grip – Essential for a Relaxed Armswing**
.... 17
    Construction and Movements of the Hand and Arm 17
    Relaxation is Necessary for Better Control 19

2   **The Grip** 23
    General Considerations 23
    Various Types of Grip 25
    The Offset Thumbhole Reexamined 28

3   **Spans and Hole Sizes** 35
    Spans 35
    Hole Sizes 37

4   **The Pitches** 39
    Middle Fingerhole Pitch 44
    Ring Fingerhole Pitch 45
    Relating Middle Fingerhole Pitch to Ring Fingerhole Pitch 46
    Thumbhole Pitch 47
    Relating Thumbhole Pitch to the Action of the Thumb 47
    Forward/Reverse Thumbhole Pitch 49
    Lateral Thumbhole Pitch 50
    One Last Word Concerning Pitch 51

5 The Release 53
Leverage – The Efficient Use of Energy 53
Some Important Elements of the Delivery 54
Relationship of Foul Line Body Position to Leverage 56
Relationship of the Grip to Leverage 57
Bowling Gloves and Wrist Supports 62
The Shoes — An Integral Part of Leverage 63
Formula for Determining the Weight of the Bowling Ball at the Point of Release (How Technical Can You Get?) 63

6 Bowling Geometrics 65
Introduction 65
Elements of the Targeting System 67
Playing Angles – The Elimination of a Popular Misconception 74
Proper Use of the Rangefinder System 76
Case 1: The 3-to-3 Target Line (Figure 23 A) 77
Case 2: The 5-to-5 Target Line (Figure 23 B) 79
Case 3: The 8-to-8 Target Line (Figure 23 C) 79
Case 4: The 12-to-10 Target Line (Figure 24 A) 80
Case 5: The 18-to-15 Target Line (Figure 24 B) 82
Case 6: The 22-to-18 Target Line (Figure 24 C) 82
The Out-to-In Target Line 83
Determining the Size of the Hook or Location of the Break When One or the Other Is Known 83
Troubleshooting the Target Line System 84
The Problem with Modern Bowling Pins 85
Some Questions to Test Your Understanding of the Targeting System 96
Answers 96
What's all of the Fuss About Shooting Spares? 97
Swing Compensation Data Form 100

Drift Compensation Data Form 101

Combining Swing And Drift Compensation Factors 102

7 Weight Distribution within a Bowling Ball 103

Personalities 103

Bowling Ball Construction 105

Use of Imbalance or Weight Center Shift........................106

Incidental Weight Shift 108

Bottom Weight 110

Top Weight..111

The Full Roller...112

Weight Block Design 114

Depth of the Weight Center 115

Drilling of Extra Holes to Shift the Weight Center 117

Loading a Bowling Ball..117

Weighing Bowling Balls...118

One Man's Meat is Another Man's Poison.....................118

8 Surface Properties of the Bowling Ball.......... 121

Hardness...122

Porosity 124

Scratches 124

Pigment in the Shell 124

Cleanliness of the Ball 125

Quality Control 125

9 Increasing Your Adaptive Range..................... 127

The Problem and Solution in Terms of Goals 128

What is an Intelligent Decision?......................................129

Variable Characteristics – A Pep Talk 130

Problems and Possible Quick Solutions 138

Case 1: The Ideal Lane Condition 143

Case 2: The Blocked Lane Condition 145

Case 3: The Neglected Lane Condition 149

Case 4: The Oil-Soaked Lane Condition 152

Case 5: The Dry Lane Condition 154

Case 6: The Synthetic Lane 155

Becoming Perceptive 156

The Serious Commitment – Give Yourself Every Opportunity 158

10 Instructions in Measuring and Drilling 161

To Drill a Strickland Offset Thumbhole Grip, Follow These Steps in the Order Presented 162

A Word On Pitch 166

A Comparison of the Standard Grip, the Strickland Offset Thumbhole Grip, and the Brunswick Offset Thumbhole Grip 166

11 Fitting the Drilled Fingertip Grip 171

Goals for Beveling and Shaping the Holes 172

Special Considerations of the Fingerholes 173

Special Considerations of the Thumbhole 174

Instructions for Beveling and Shaping the Holes 175

A Final Word 181

Recommended Reading 183

Glossary 189

Preface

Thank you, dear bowler, for choosing to read my book! Writing *Perceptive Bowling* has been personally gratifying, and I hope that my efforts will help you get more enjoyment out of the sport that I dearly love. Before you get started, please let me tell you something very important about the purpose of this book.

Perceptive Bowling is not intended to be an introductory text! it was developed in response to the requirements of the aspiring bowler who has reached a plateau and who finds that basic texts do not give him (or her) the insights necessary for further improvement. Over the years, I eagerly awaited the publication of just such a book, but no such book ever appeared on the market. So, I just had to pick up what information I could from various sources – conversations with getter bowlers, with pro shop operators, with proprietors, with instructors, as wall as from many hours of personal, on-lane experience. I can assure you that I scratched and struggled to develop successful formulas for the many different bowling conditions. This process takes a long time unless training is supervised by a competent instructor on many different lane conditions. This option is simply unavailable to most bowlers (especially those in the hundreds of small towns in America). To further complicate matters, everyone who bowls considers himself a teacher, and these people are unwitting false prophets who spread untruths in well-intentioned ways. Taking all of these considerations into account, I felt that it was my responsibility to sit down and write a better bowling book.

What information should be included and what should be left out? Well, look at it this way. If I had written a book that said the same thing as every other book, but in a different way, I would be simply kidding myself and would be doing nothing to advance the sport. You

5

do not need to be take back to the same old starting point; you need fresh material – something relevant and tested. I wanted to discuss concepts that needed further discussion, but I did not want to include the redundant filler that has appeared in just about every bowling book that has been published over the years (i.e. entire chapters devoted to the proper attire, how to keep score, ABC rules, bowling etiquette, blank score sheets, etc.). Such information is fine, but it is available elsewhere; more important subjects must be dealt with, and I give my attention to these.

I have developed this book in an orderly fashion, from the simple to the more complex, in a way that will enable you to establish a mental framework upon which you can build from your own experience. The table of contents gives an overview.

In the first four chapters, the hand, arm, and fit of the ball are thoroughly discussed before a consideration of the release in chapter five. It is this chapter that deals with the interrelatedness of all of the factors discussed to that point. Chapter six is a reevaluation of the Rangefinder targeting system, and it is a personalized treatment of how the delivery relates to different playing angles. Chapters seven and eight deal with the variable characteristics of the bowling ball, and they provide the reader with information necessary to understand chapter nine. I feel that chapter nine is the most important chapter, because it gives you the rudiments of a formula for playing all lane conditions by manipulating all of the variables discussed in previous chapters; it is the chapter that "puts it all together", so to speak! Chapters ten and eleven give instructions in the drilling and fitting of the bowling ball — information that I have never before seen in a form easily read by the general bowling public. Finally, the "Recommended Reading" section is annotated to that readers may easily find information elsewhere when necessary. **Perceptive Bowling** is analogous to specialized books that have already been written about golf and tennis, therefore, I feel this book is long overdue.

I have chosen the title, **Perceptive Bowling**, because what I have attempted to do is provide the reader with enough information to make him more aware of his bowling environment so that he can learn for himself at a greatly accelerated rate. Bowling costs about one dollar per game nowadays, and more thoughtful application during practice is necessary to make the most out of the session without spending a small fortune. The concepts that I have discussed can help anyone, regardless of average. If you are an experienced bowler, I believe you can still increase your capabilities by being more aware (i.e. more perceptive), even if you have not been able to improve for what seems to be a long period of time.

Again, let me say that I appreciate your confidence in choosing my book. Further, I would be interested in hearing from you regarding how this book has helped you, or regarding anything you may not understand. Contact me via e-mail at bob@roberthstrickland.com.

Yours for more perceptive bowling,

Bob Strickland, 1980

Addendum to Preface

When first published, **Perceptive Bowling** was considered groundbreaking because it was the first bowling text for serious bowlers that included thorough consideration of the following topics:

- A study of the action of the hand and arm
- Explanation of the relationship between the grip and swing tension
- Review of several grip types with respect to their efficiency
- Detailed information about span, hole size, and pitch
- A study of the finish position, the release, and leverage
- Detailed information on targeting, various target lines
- A review of bowling ball design and weight distribution
- Discussion of bowling ball surface properties
- How to adapt to various types of lane condition
- Instructions in drilling the offset thumbhole grip
- Instructions on contouring and beveling the grip holes

It was the first book to give insight into ways to use hand position and ball selection to cope with lane conditions and to use ball cleaner during competition. It was useful to all serious bowlers in 1980, and the lessons herein, in addition to being historically interesting, are useful today.

Bob Strickland, 2011

8

Acknowledgements

I thank my parents for showing me the value of always taking the proper direction and pursuing the goal of excellence. To the late Wilkie Burns of Newark, Delaware, I must give the warmest thanks for instilling in me the confidence and optimism that is essential if one is to be successful at anything. His faith in my bowling capabilities and in my potential in life did a wealth of good for my self-image, and I shall always be grateful to him for it. He was the type of person whom others seek out because of his ability to show anyone the bright side of any situation; he was truly one-of-a-kind.

To the following persons in whose pro shops I developed my craft, I reaffirm my gratitude and friendship:

> Rex Blair, Dallas Texas
>
> Jim Hensley, Austin, Texas
>
> Ken Cousson, Athens, Georgia
>
> John Vavala, Jr., Wilmington, Delaware
>
> Kirk Kinnamon, Portland, Oregon
>
> Al Flores, Wilmington, California
>
> Bob Stiles, Houston, Texas
>
> Bob Tomlinson and Roy "Pete" Moore, Dallas Texas
>
> Earl Pichette and Clint Hunter, Dallas, Texas

And, thanks are in order to the following folks whose advice, stories, counseling, and fellowship helped my along the way: J. B. Solomon, Bob Potts, Pat Wood, Gene Loomis, Bob Boulden, Johnny Cerminaro, Mike McKamy, Bob Talley, Buddy Bomar, Cecil Caddel,

Roy Mantle, Bill Taylor, Dawson Taylor, Pete Carter, Joe Joseph, Carmen Salvino, Bill Lillard, Joe Norris, Gary Brewer, Jerry Essick, Phil Cox, Keith Little, Alta Little, Jean Padilla, and the absolutely **great** guys who bowl in the Sunday afternoon Portland, Oregon Traveling League, and those wonderful folks tho make a second home of Cecil Lanes in Elkton, Maryland!

Thanks to Melvin Powers, Wilshire Publishing Company (9731 Variel Avenue, Chatsworth, California 91311-4315) for allowing me to use excerpts from the book *How You Can Bowl Better Using Self-Hypnosis*. More acknowledgements appear throughout the book and I am sure that I have not mentioned everyone who has given me help in writing this book. However, I must give a special thanks to my Cairn Terrier, Mac, who waited patiently by my side during the entire project.

A Fond Remembrance

I will never forget two colorful figures whose barnstorming efforts during the great bowling boom of the late 50's help to elevate the sport to the family recreational activity that it is today. These men are the great Steve Nagy and the equally great Billy Welu! They represented the essence of professionalism at all times — love and deep respect for their chosen endeavor.

Steve was a powerful man who threw the ball with the authority of a freight train. If he lost a match, he would often take off his belt and whip the offending ball. If he won, he sometimes offered to drain the "sour juice" out of his opponent's ball with a jury-rigged spigot inserted into the thumbhole. I have seen Steve deliver his ball and then jump into a spectator seat in time to see the ball hit the pins. He was a complete showman, but he was a terrific bowler — the first, in fact, to bowl a perfect game on a filmed bowling series! The PBA sportsmanship award bears his name; this speaks for itself.

Billy was a stylist with the best form, balance, and leverage of any bowler I have ever seen. He was well-known for his openness and generosity, and he was always the first to start a conversation. He often kept up a lightening-punch stream of chatter that showed the warmth and humor characteristic of a Southern gentleman. As the color expert along with Chris Schenkel on the American Broadcasting Company's PBA Tour telecasts, Billy added tremendously to the audience awareness.

Steve and Billy were champions in life as well as in sports. Bowling would not have fared as well without them; likewise, I feel bowling is not the same without them.

Introduction

Perception is the ability to be aware of the environment through observation and understanding. The learning process begins with the ability of the learner to perceive, and self-improvement in any skill can be greatly accelerated by the development of greater perception of the various components of the skill. This line of reasoning can be extended to bowling since the bowler's environment includes all facets of the sport such as the pins, the approaches, the lanes, and, of course, the equipment he uses. These are usually explained in some detail in existing bowling instruction manuals. However, my book will deal with topics, a thorough understanding of which is necessary for the aspiring bowler to improve.

Most existing bowling manuals seem to take the reader only so far and fail to instruct further. The unfortunate result is that there are few advanced bowling texts on the market. There are many reasons for this deficiency, not the least of which is the reluctance of many companies to publish a text that they feel will not have mass appeal. In my opinion, this belief is unfounded for several reasons. First, the modern bowler appears to be a well-informed, thinking individual. This conclusion is reinforced by results of a study conducted by the Target Group Index and commissioned by the National Bowling Council. They found that the largest group of bowlers is young — between 17 and 34. Further, almost 16 million bowlers (approximately 40% of all bowlers) have attended college, the largest group being of the professional/managerial type. These figures indicate that an impressive number of bowlers are persons who can and will profit from a greater understanding of their chosen sport. The game is not simple anymore; the days are gone when one ball could be used on all lane conditions. Bowlers have not kept up with their counterparts in golf and tennis as far as useful knowledge of various aspects of their sport is concerned, and this book will attempt to bring them up to that level.

Secondly, although many of the concepts that I discuss are commonly known by professionals in the sport, no previous author has presented these ideas in a single publication. Many young and/or aspiring bowlers who have mastered the text-outlined fundamentals but who do not reside in highly competitive bowling areas have no quick, inexpensive means of obtaining this essential information.

Thirdly, hundreds of non-professionals fit and drill their own bowling balls. Even though they have access to drilling instruction manuals, they may neither understand the sketchy, incomplete language nor question the arbitrary methods described. Consequently, the bowler may never really understand the all-important process involved in fitting and drilling the equipment that he uses every time he bowls. Even if he does not drill his own balls, the bowler **as a consumer** needs to know how to communicate his ideas to his professional driller. Most important, he needs to know how to spot an inept driller so he does not waste his money and time on poor quality equipment.

Finally, for the sport to advance, there need to be more well-distributed bowling texts made available to the bowling community. New lane conditions emerge with advances in technology. New bowling balls are constantly being developed to help the bowler cope with these new conditions. The intellect of the bowling community must grow to sensibly utilize this new equipment for enhanced enjoyment of the sport. Basic texts have done a fine job in explaining fundamentals, but there comes a time in the skill attainment process when these basics no longer satisfy our needs. I hope this book, in addition to partially fulfilling the needs of serious bowlers, will prompt the writing of other advanced bowling texts.

I have deliberated for a long time about the proper sequence of presentation of the subject matter of this book. Finally, I decided that no sequence would be satisfactory. Why? Because the bowling ball as it appears sitting on the ball return or on the floor is one concept in itself. In the absence of the hand, arm, and body, the bowling ball is a lifeless entity that has no importance in itself and bears no relationship to the bowler.

When the ball is picked up, the fingers inserted into the holes, and the ball used in the actual bowling delivery, the grip becomes part of a complex system resulting from the interplay of human and inanimate characteristics. Analysis of this system cannot have a beginning, a middle, and ending as an organized presentation must have. The system is a continuum; it is composed of interconnected parts, each of which must be functioning properly if the system is to function properly.

A discussion of this system is necessarily circular, the explanation of one part being dependent upon an understanding of another. *To assign a structure to this book must be arbitrary, therefore, and I hope that the one that I have chosen will allow you to establish a mental framework upon which you yourself can build.* As you learn more detail about each of the concepts from bowling experience, the framework will grow more complete, giving you the knowledge that has sometimes taken years for even the most intelligent bowlers to attain.

I have chosen not to discuss certain topics in this volume for two reasons. First, many of the topics are discussed adequately in existing texts. Perhaps more detail about these subjects will be appropriate later when further technological advances pertaining to them are made. Second, I have to limit my discuss to subjects I feel are sorely in need of explanation. These concepts are usually omitted from bowling manuals, and they need prime consideration. Of course, I want to express my opinions, but I will try to give other opinions an objective review. I hope that readers who hold strong similar or different opinions will take the time to collect their own thoughts and write them down for all of us to enjoy and evaluate. In this way, all of us who love the sport can grow more proficient through increased awareness and can become more perceptive bowlers.

Figure 1: Movement of the Hand at the Wrist

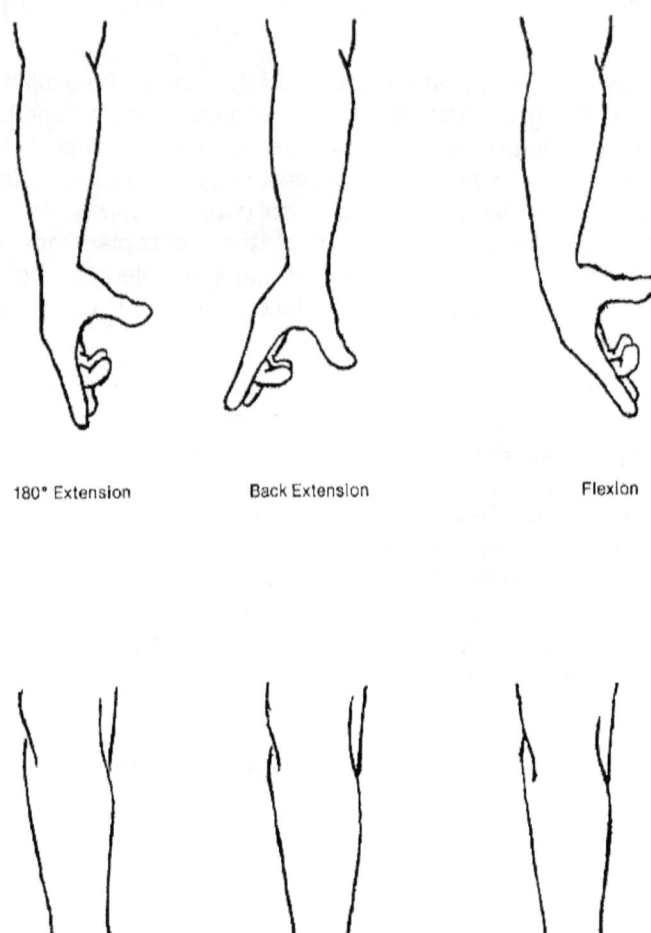

1 A Proper Grip – Essential for a Relaxed Armswing

Construction and Movements of the Hand and Arm

Muscles can only contract, therefore they can only pull. Thus, for an extremity to move back and forth, it must be attached to two sets of muscles, each opposed to the other. Further, the size of a muscle mass (the number of individual muscle fibers it contains) will determine the load it is capable of handling. Some simple terms that apply to movements of the hand are shown in Figure 1. When the fingers and thumb are flexed, the end result is a fist; when the wrist is flexed, the result is commonly called a cupped wrist. A 180-degree extension of the fingers and wrist makes a perfectly straight plane from the elbow to the tip of the fingers as the arm is viewed with the thumb toward the observer.

The **flexion-extension** movement is responsible for adjusting the amount of lift that the fingers can apply to the ball. Looking at the back of the hand, one can see that there are other directions of movement called **adduction** and **abduction**. These movements are extremely important to the effectiveness of the roll of the ball due to their influence on the axis of rotation of the track. These movements are independent of flexion and extension, and combinations of all of these movements can be made to adjust the position of the hand during the swing and release. Please take a few moments to become familiar with these terms as they will be important to an understanding of the release that will be discussed later. Demonstrate these movements to yourself and see how they affect you. Try them with and without a ball in your hand (you should experiment with every concept outlined in this book, anyway).

What should one strive for in the bowling grip? A simple answer would be *maximum power with minimum effort*. Power does not mean the bowler must maintain a death grip on the ball. On the contrary, such a grip would require tension of just about every muscle of the hand and forearm and many of those of the upper arm. Most people also think that stretching the grip spans as far as they can stand is the way to achieve power. This idea is also incorrect and is in opposition to the attainment of power.

Consider the hand. It is made up of two muscle systems — a group serving the fingers and a group serving the thumb. This point is illustrated in Figure 2. In addition to those shown, there are muscles in between the joints to allow for the curl of the fingers (flexion). The muscles that allow for flexion of the fingers at the base are the abductors and adductors. These muscles also allow for the tilting of the fingers toward and away from the thumb, respectively; and they can come under tremendous strain in the bowling grip unless special compensations (proper pitch orientations) are made for them. Notice that the finger muscles lie on the long plane of the hand, while the muscle mass of the thumb lies on a plane approximately 90-degrees opposed to them. Figure 3 shows that some of the muscles that flex the fingers are located all of the way up in the forearm and are attached to points on or near the elbow. The wrist in this drawing is, incidentally, held in the 180-degree extended, slightly abducted position.

Figure 2: The Muscle Systems of the Hand – The muscle mass of the thumb is roughly ninety degrees to the abductor and adductor muscles of the fingers.

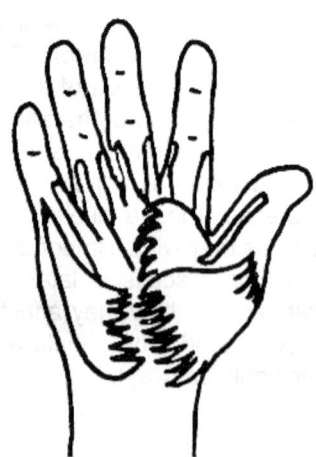

We grip the ball with both systems of hand muscles. These muscles are integrated with the muscles of the forearm. Therefore, *one cannot consider the hand alone in determining the fit of the bowling ball.* Further, relative relaxation of the upper arm cannot be achieved without relative relaxation of the muscles of the forearm and hand. *Test this yourself.* Tense the hand and keep the forearm relaxed. Next, tense the forearm and keep the muscles of the upper arm relaxed (if you can do this you deserve a prize). In a very pointed way, the bowling grip must be made to accommodate minimum tension of the hand muscles so that there will be no unnecessary strain in the arm.

There is a particular orientation of each muscle mass so that it can exert maximum pull with the least effort. This orientation depends on the points of insertion of the muscles on the bones to which they are attached. Teams of muscles can be developed according to this principle to attain the desired power in the grip with the least wear and tear on the muscles involved. This is called developing proper muscle balance. The bowling ball grip can either interfere with or encourage the development of this balance depending on the correctness of pitch, spans, and the contour of the holes.

Relaxation is Necessary for Better Control

Relaxation of the bowling grip is quite different from total relaxation. If we totally relaxed all of our muscles while standing, we would fall down. Likewise, if we totally relaxed our hand and arm muscles while holding a bowling ball at our side, we would (and should) drop it. Some muscles are always at work; the question is how many are necessary to do the required work. Relaxation of the bowling grip is, then, the ability of the muscle teams to accommodate the force of the ball throughout the swing with a minimum amount of tension. Strictly, what this means is that a lesser number of individual muscle fibers are contracting at the same time. Each muscle mass involved does not completely contract, rather it contracts partially, the least numbers of the fibers being called into action. If the muscles have been balanced properly through intelligent practice, exercise, and use of the appropriate grip, minimum effort wlll get the job done. As a simplistic illustration, if it takes 2500 muscle flbers on one slde of the bone to flex an arm that is holding a bowling ball and 2500 flbers on the other side opposed to the first set to balance the flexing action, why should the lack of a proper grip on the ball promote the use of

5000 fibers on each side to accomplish the same task? A poorly-fitting bowling ball, as most seem to be, can help to condition or train a bowler's arm and hand to be more tense in the swing. He is then subject to all of the problems brought about by a tense swing — deviating swing, inconsistent release, poor coordination, etc.

Why do I feel that the grip is so important? I think that two exceptional books influenced my opinion on this subject One, *The Secret of Bowling Strikes* by Dawson Taylor, dealt with the swing and release in a unique way, and provided the inspiration for my discussion of the influence of the grip in the release. The other book, *How You Can Bowl Better Using Self-hypnosis*, by Jack Heise, stressed the importance of relaxation for better control of the bowling form. Heise shows, step-by-step, the method of using self-hypnosis to relegate all of the mechanics of the bowling delivery to the subconscious mind so that the conscious mind can be completely free to be directed to the target. He explains, "When automatic movements are made, they are controlled subconsciously. Your conscious mind does not interfere, and there is no conflict set up that creates tension."

It is my contention that *imperfect fit of the bowling grip is the major cause of interference with the relaxation of the hand and arm*. To eliminate the swing as a source of interference with concentration on the target, the swing must be relatively relaxed. Authors of bowling manuals say something like, "Choose a well-fitting ball." or "Go to a pro shop and purchase a custom-fitted ball." The truth is that a great majority of bowling balls do not fit the hands of their owners well enough. This is true even for some of the best bowlers who seem to succeed in spite of this limitation. I feel that they could be even better if they had a more precisely-fitted grip. If you find this statement hard to believe, look at the unnecessary callouses on the hands of your local better bowlers. Ask them if their thumbs swell or if their hands hurt during the first few deliveries of a bowling session. See if they have thick cuticles on their fingers.

If you learn nothing else from my book, please learn that *the only way one can relax the hand and arm in the swing is to be totally confident that the ball will be secure during the swing and that the hand will release the ball only at the proper point (the explosion point)*. One may be convinced that the ball is perfectly controlled during the swing and release, and hence may be blaming errors in release on timing difficulties. In fact, the timing may simply be dependent upon grip difficulties. Heise states, "The cause of tension is fear. If you tighten the muscles in your hand and arm, the muscles tire easily....when fear produces tension, even though you may be unaware of the source (italics mine), the muscles can remain taut...." I think that fear of losing the ball is a major problem. The ball may be slipping off the hand so slightly during the swing that it may not be apparent to the bowler. His subconscious will detect this, and the swing will become slightly tense, thereby defeating the purpose of relaxation. Further, I believe that my modification of the offset thumbhole grip is the most correct grip layout for the normal human hand, and even this one must be tooled or worked out with utmost care to insure the optimum fit. Only with this perfection can the swing become truly relaxed.

Relaxation, as Jack Heise defines it, and as I have related it to the bowling grip, is the effortless, subconscious control of well-balanced muscles of the hand and arm. Only the minimum degree of muscle flexion should be needed to hold the ball throughout the swing. The muscles are then able to spring into action to accommodate the added tension requirement of the release, which is more than just a continuance of the swing. Only well-balanced, toned muscles can come into action subconsciously at the exact time with consistency, and the bowling grip can make or break the development of the subconsciously-controlled swing and release. Keeping this idea in mind, let us turn to a consideration of grips.

Figure 3: The Muscle System of the Forearm Showing Tendons Leading to the Fingers (FT)

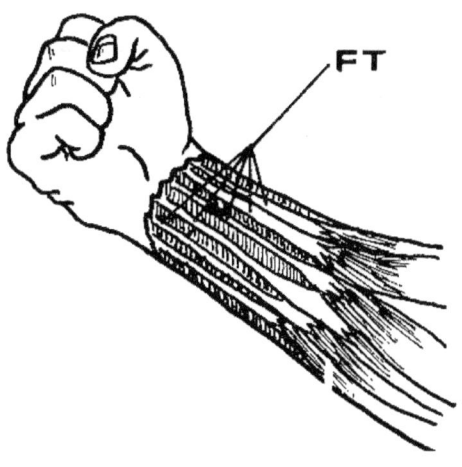

Figure 4: A Typical Grip Layout Measurement Sheet (Courtesy of Roy "Pete" Moore and Bob Tomlinson)

Bowling Ball Order

Customer _____ Phone _____
Street _____
City _____ State _____ Zip _____

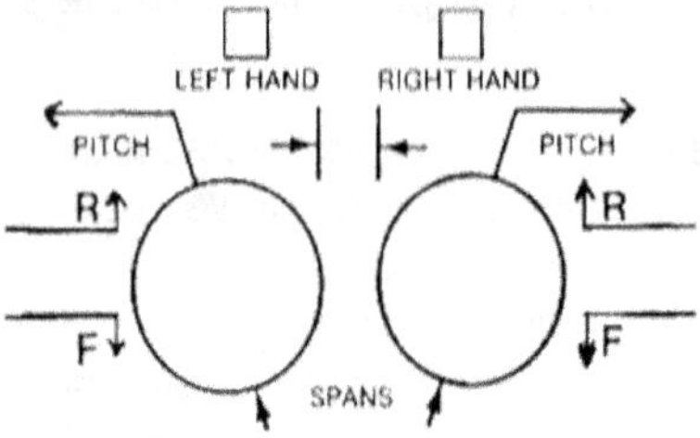

☐ LEFT HAND   ☐ RIGHT HAND
PITCH — R↑ — F↓   PITCH — ↑R — ↓F
SPANS

F↑ — PITCH — R↓
SIDE PITCH

TYPE OF DRILLING:
☐ Conventional
☐ Modified Offset
☐ Full Offset
☐ Finger Tip
☐ Semi-Finger Tip
☐ _____

SPECIAL INSTRUCTIONS:
☐   1st ____ 2nd ____
_____
_____

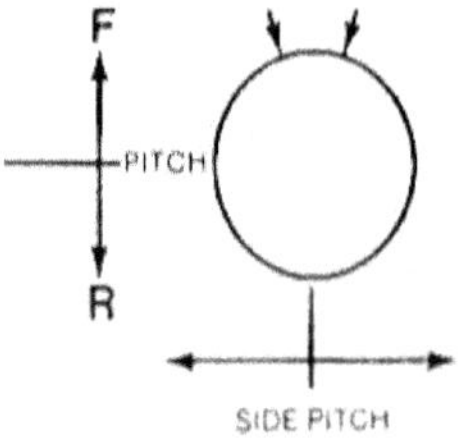

BALL IDENTIFICATION
Color _____
Weight _____
Initials _____
Ball No. _____

Weight Distribution:

Top _____
Side _____ P   N
Finger _____
Thumb _____
Bottom _____

Durometric Hardness _____
Invoice No. _____
Ship To: ☐ Establishment ☐ Customer
Ship Via: ☐ Parcel Post   ☐ Express
☐ Prepaid   ☐ C.O.D.   ☐ Charge

ACCEPTANCE OF SPECIFICATIONS
& CHARGES

Customer's
Signature _____
Date _____

2 The Grip

General Considerations

Figure 4 (facing page) is an example of the grip measurement forms used by virtually every driller to record the twelve measurements necessary to properly fit a bowling ball to a customer's hand. Two measurements, the **spans** (the distances between the leading edges of the thumbhole and each of the fingerholes), are the easiest to obtain accurately, but they are the most freely abused in practice. The next in ease of obtaining accuracy, the **hole sizes**, are normally fitted too large. The next measurements, the **pitches** (the degree of directedness of the axis of the hole toward or away from the geometric center of the ball) are left almost completely to the discretion of the driller because the customer probably does not know his pitch requirement. In truth, the driller probably does not know it either, but this will become apparent to you as you progress through the book. The final measurement, that of the **web** or **bridge** (the space between the fingerholes) will be either a predetermined width or too wide because of the manufacturers requirement of a minimum 1/4" bridge for the ball guarantee to be effective. I will discuss the limitations of each of these measurements and review some of the current theories in subsequent chapters. For purposes of this introduction, however, I will limit my discussion to briefer comments.

Spans: The spans are the easiest to measure accurately, but in most cases they are fitted too wide. Sometimes this error is as much as 5/16" in a fingertip grip. I really do not know of a good reason for this error, but I would guess that what the driller is attempting to do is flatten the fingers onto the surface of the ball while the bowler has his hand firmly seated in the grip. Flatness of the fingers on the ball is not a valid criterion of correct fit. Many bowlers seem to think that this is a desirable effect because the stretching makes the grip feel powerful. Actually, this stretch has no positive influence on power at the release point, and it is rather a good indicator of excessive span.

(*Author's Note:* In the last 30 years, the trend in fitting has been to make spans too short. Even with the wealth of information available today, many drillers continue to be "timid" when fitting spans. One reason for this is that they do not require the customer to exercise the hand before fitting, thereby loosening the muscles for a more accurate determination. Further, they do not adequately stretch the fingers over the measuring device, with the thumb fully inserted in the thumbhole of the device.)

Hole Sizes: I feel strongly that the sizes of beginning finger and thumb holes should be rather small because, for proper fit, smaller holes must be tooled or worked out to give them the proper shape or contour. Nobody's fingers are round, and round holes are drilled only because the machines cannot drill properly-shaped holes for the fingers.

Pitches: The pitches of the fingerholes must be considered separately from that of the thumbhole because, as I have explained, the fingers and thumb are serviced by two separate muscle systems. It is my opinion that, for a three-hole grip, there should be at least four and probably *six* planes of pitch for the grip (a forward/reverse and a lateral plane for each hole) instead of the two that are offered by the standard drilling. **Pitches of the fingerholes are more valuable in achieving comfort of the grip and proper leverage than in changing the roll characteristics of the ball.** The characteristics are more successfully altered by changing the pitches of the thumbhole. Spans are closely related to pitches, and a greater understanding of this relationship is needed to predict a more correct grip for a particular hand.

Bridge: The size of the bridge should be determined by the distance between the fingers at the point they would enter the holes if one were actually holding the ball. In other words, the driller should measure the distance between the fingers as the customer is simulating a grip. This would give a rough idea of the necessary size of the bridge but, even then, the edges of the bridge should be tooled for comfort. Excessively wide bridges can wear on the insides of the fingers but a too-narrow bridge will not allow for much variation in fingerhole pitches due to the chance of running the holes together at the bottom.

Various Types of Grip

I want to show you only some of the infinite variations of grips used by famous and non-famous bowlers down through the years. *Note that the clockface orientation reference (explained fully in the chapter on pitch) is used in* Figure 5. Note also that a line drawn from 12 o'clock to 6 o'clock on the circumference of the ball divides the ball into two equal halves. This line is called the **centerline**, and is usually the beginning of any grip layout used by a driller. The letters used in Figure 5 correspond to those used in the text.

A. **The Two-finger Grip**: This was the first attempt at a true grip. Before this, bowlers simply palmed a holeless ball. (Count Gengler is said to have been the most proficient.) The holes were directed toward the geometric center of the ball (termed zero pitch) and the span extended from the base of the thumb to the bend of the middle finger at the second joint. Bowers using this grip were successful because a powerfully-rolling ball was not an asset on the shellac-finished lanes common at the times. There existed a deep, visibly darker, track from the foul line to the right-hand pocket area, and to hit the pocket was a matter of consistently placing a slow or medium speed ball within the confines of this track. A powerful ball (such as a fingertip ball with more speed and lift) would simply fight the tendency of the track to direct the ball. Actually the two-finger grip was just about the only one known. It was easy for machinists (there were no pro shops) to drill on standard drill presses, and two fingers seemed to be enough to hold the ball. Ed Lubanski is one of the last to use the two finger grip.

Figure 5: Various Types of Grip

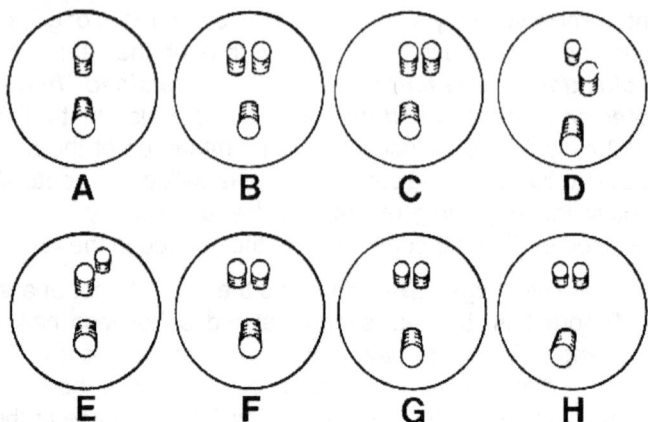

B. ***The Standard Three-hole Conventional Grip***: This grip features the thumbhole superimposed on the circumferential centerline with the fingerholes placed on either side of this line. The fingerholes are usually drilled (pitched) parallel with each other, and the spans are the distances between the base of the thumb and the second joints of each finger. This grip as well as any other standard grip features only two planes of pitch. (This point may not mean much now, but remember this for future reference — forward/reverse pitch for both fingerholes and the thumbhole are parallel with a plane made by the grip layout centerline. The lateral pitches are perpendicular to this centerline plane, **hence only two planes of pitch for all three holes.** If this it not clear to you, forget this notion until you read the chapter on pitch.) The three-finger grip was developed to minimize the strain caused by the two-finger conventional grip. Bill Lillard and Glenn Allison still use the three-hole conventional grip.

C. ***The Collier Grip***: This grip is essentially a two-finger grip with a ring fingerhole added. It is actually a change in pitch relationship from the standard three-hole grip because the spans may remain the same. The Collier grip was developed to relieve the strain put against the bridge side of the middle finger by the standard drilling by moving the fingerholes so that the middle fingerhole is also superimposed on the centerline, as is the thumbhole. Obviously, the feel of this grip will be quite different from a standard drilling of the exact spans, hole sizes, and forward/reverse pitches because the planes of reference of pitch have been changed. One of my favorites, Johnny King, uses the Collier grip.

(*Author's Note:* Zero lateral pitch of the thumbhole feels like it is pointed away from the palm; therefore a quicker release is obtained. To achieve the feel of zero lateral pitch, the thumbhole must be angled approximately 1/8 inch under the palm.)

D. *The Sarge Easter Grip*: This grip was devised by Ebber "Sarge" Easter, an amazing man, who past 60 years of age won the national doubles title with Ed Lubanski. Its design featured a centerline thumbhole and a centerline fingertip middle fingerhole span (to the bend of the first joint). A conventional-span ring fingerhole was added. Billy Welu and Billy Golembiewski used modifications of this basic layout.

E. *The Chic Grip*: This grip featured a centerline thumbhole and conventional centerline middle fingerhole with a fingertip span ring fingerhole added. It was devised to lessen strain on the middle finger while maximizing lift with the ring finger. The great Steve Nagy sometimes used this grip.

F. *The Standard Semifingertip Grip*: This grip incorporates the same relationships as the standard three-hole conventional grip except that the spans extend to somewhere between the first and second joints of the fingers to the base of the thumb. In my opinion, this grip is useless. It was originally designed to produce more leverage than the conventional grip while retaining the turn or spin potential. Likewise, it could provide more turn than the fingertip grip. It must have been unsuccessful because it is a very uncommon grip today, although it has been used by almost every good bowler at some time in his bowling experience.

I feel that the conventional grip provides the best turn at the release and the fingertip grip gives the best lifting potential. The inability to decide how deep to place the fingers in the semifingertip grip can lead to problems of stretching the hand. This can allow for pulling the thumb out of the thumbhole during the swing, and this is a highly undesirable effect. My advice is to avoid this grip.

G. **The Standard Fingertip Grip**: This is the most common grip used by better bowlers today. It gives the greatest amount of lift of any of the standard grips, and lift is needed an modern lane surfaces. The spans extend from the base of a centerline-placed thumb to the bend of the first joint of the fingers.

H. **The Offset Thumbhole Grip**: The original Brunswick offset thumbhole grip called for the thumbhole to be positioned with its edge 1/4" to the left of the centerline. The pitch of the fingers was adjusted so that the fingers (for a right handed grip) would point awkwardly to the fleshy part of the hand opposite the side of the thumb. Strictly, the offset thumb grip says nothing about the pitch of the fingerholes, and one may offset the thumbhole to any degree. The essential feature of this grip is that the thumbhole is placed in a position closer to the base of the thumb before the spans are chosen. Note that the offset thumbhole can be used with any combination of spans and pitches as long as the thumbhole is not superimposed on the centerline and as long as the fingerholes are placed on either side of the centerline. This grip has fallen into disuse for what I feel are invalid reasons, and these will be discussed in the following section.

(**Author's Note:** Measured zero lateral thumbhole pitch feels like it is pointed more toward the palm than in the standard layout; offering the possibility of a more secure grip is for those whose base thumb joint has sufficient range of motion. To achieve the feel of zero lateral pitch in this Brunswick version, the thumbhole must be angled approximately 1/8 to 1/4 inch away from the palm. This is an extreme measure, though, and I do not really care for this degree of offset because it actually feels loose in the hand.)

The Offset Thumbhole Reexamined

My own modification of this (Strickland offset thumbhole grip, see *A Comparison of the Standard Grip, the Strickland Offset Thumbhole Grip, and the Brunswick Offset Thumbhole Grip*) requires placement of each fingerhole equidistant to and on opposite sides of the grip layout centerline. The thumbhole is placed the proper distance from each fingerhole and tangent to, neither superimposed on nor a great distance away from, the centerline. Figure 6 illustrates this concept. After studying the two right-handed grips in Figure 6 for a while, you may say to yourself, "There's no difference between A and B! This is the essence of the problem. Drillers continue to simply turn the entire grip slightly and declare it to have an offset thumbhole!

Figure 6: In A, the thumbhole is tangent to the centerline; in B, it is superimposed on the centerline. Span M equals span X; span R equals span Y.

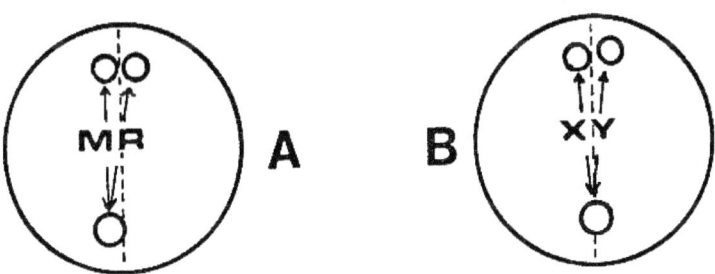

In fact, one prominent author and bowling researcher calls the offset grip an imaginary, non-existent grip layout.

(*Author's Note:* This gentleman became my teacher, advocate, and friend, but we silently remained in disagreement about the reality of the offset thumbhole grip.)

His attitude is based on the notion that the spans lie on the circumference of the ball anyway, and therefore no matter where the holes are placed, the grips are the same if the spans are the same. **This line of reasoning is correct only if one completely disregards the relationship of the thumbhole and fingerhole pitches to each other and the direction that the ball pulls on the arm during the swing and release!**

If one takes these factors into consideration, grips A and B are worlds apart! Figure 7 shows this difference in a two-dimensional way. Refer, if necessary, to the different perspectives and clockface terminology explained in the chapter on pitch. If we assume extreme forward fingerhole pitch (toward the thumb) and that the fingerholes are parallel with each other for the sake of illustration, it is easy to see that in grip A, the forward pitch of the middle fingerhole is directed more toward the thumbhole, rather than to the left of it.

Figure 7: Label View of Three Different Grips (note clockface reference)

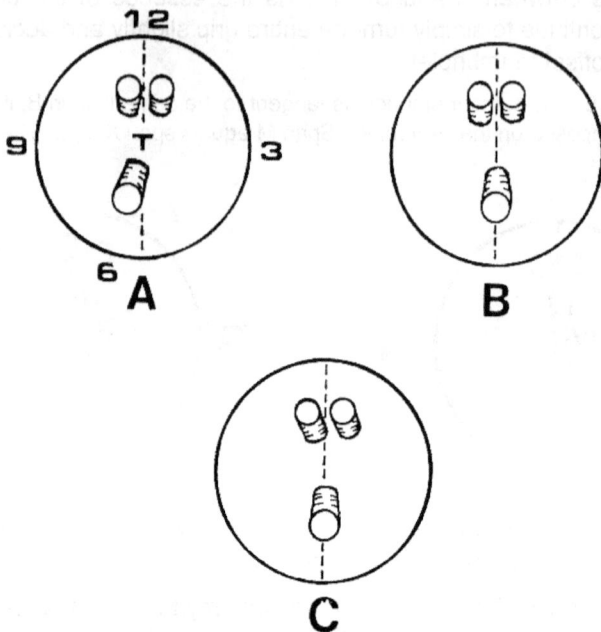

This grip is kinesiologically sound because it approximates the actual closing action of the hand. *Test this yourself.* Look at your open palm and slowly simulate making the bowling grip. *Notice that even when the hand is completely closed the middle finger will he directed toward the base of the thumb and never toward the web of flesh between the thumb and forefinger as the standard grip B necessitates.* Beginning with a layout such as grip B, the driller may feel that he can simulate the same feel as grip A by manipulating lateral fingerhole pitches as in grip C. This is not valid, either, because the relationship of the thumb pitch to that of the fingers is different in grip C from grip A.

(*Author's Note:* One cannot simply direct the fingerholes away from the base of the thumbhole and claim that the grip is "offset." The forward/reverse plane of the thumbhole must also be moved away from the bridge, toward the middle fingerhole! The thumbhole pitches, even if measured zero all around in Grips A and C, do not feel the same. Hence, the grips are different!.)

This relationship is another reason that grip A differs from grip B. Consider Figure 8 in which the three balls of Figure 7 have been rotated so that the 6 o'clock position of the ball is toward the observer. The pitch relationship differences then become obvious. This point was explained to me initially by Al Flores, an excellent ball driller and friend from Wilmington, California. (incidentally, Al is the only person who has drilled a bowling ball for me since I began drilling for myself in 1964).

Figure 8: View of Three Grips with the Label at the Top (T)

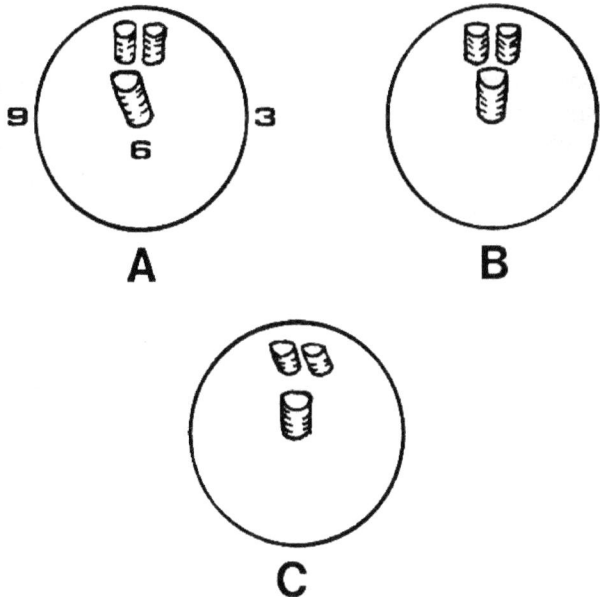

I believe that the thumbhole, unlike the Brunswick offset grip, should be no predetermined distance from the grip centerline. Rather, and arbitrarily, I must admit, *I have chosen to offset it one radius from the centerline, hence tangent to the centerline*. This is an attempt to accommodate the different sizes of thumbholes and their probable relationship to the length of the span. The tangent position seems more sensible than a greater offset (like the Brunswick version) that allows more wobble of the grip in the swing. I have what I feel are good, sound reasons for my version of the offset grip and its value in promoting security of the swing and leverage in the release. These topics and detailed drilling instructions will be included in later chapters. Why was the offset thumb grip abandoned? One reason is that no one really knew what the grip was or they had a sketchy idea of what it was. Another is that the Brunswick version was really a very insecure grip that gave a very fast, sometimes premature release of the ball. Probably the best reason is illustrated by a short story.

Originally, grips were drilled on a straight drill press. Drillers were persons who, in addition to their love of bowling, were very familiar with the characteristics of machine tools. As bowling became more popular, the demand for faster service in providing drilled bowling balls became a major concern. Christmas rushes didn't help the situation then, and they are still the primary source of many unused, ill-fitting bowling balls. Discount houses and department stores saw an opportunity to make money on the sale of balls, bags, and shoes, with many of these being of poor structural quality. Consequently, as more people purchased their own equipment, the more inexperienced sales clerks became so-called trained, or expert ball drillers who fitted and drilled so-called custom-fitted balls.

Often, even bowling establishments would (and still do) allow inexperienced persons to drill balls for paying customers. With greater demand for product and the employment of unskilled drillers came the invention of semiautomated drilling machines that could be set to drill the entire ball (all of the holes) by making some adjustments and without moving the ball in the holding cradle. These adjustments can be made according to cookbook-type directions that do not tax the driller to figure out what he is doing!

I do not mean to say that anyone drilling a ball on these machines should be suspect. Obviously, the machines are as accurate as their operators. However, I do offer some criticisms of these machines. First, they are set up to drill only two planes of pitch based on the centerline plane of reference. Through a series of combinations of pitch adjustment and turning the ball in the holding cradle, they can be made to drill offset holes etc., but such adjustments are exceptions to the normal directions included with the machines. In other words, these machines operate on the assumption that the hand needs only two planes of pitch. The Brunswick Gil-Mac is almost impossible to see into without the aid of a flashlight, and the AMF automated machine is normally set to drill one fingerhole first, then the thumbhole, and then the other fingerhole (no provision for properly offsetting the thumbhole first)

These machines are designed for speed, and I feel that speed and accuracy are incompatible. Besides, these machines cost from three to eight times as much as a completely outfitted (but slower) drill press. The ability to remeasure and correct mistakes while drilling the ball is a definite advantage. Truly this takes time, but speed of drilling is not even a consideration when accurate drilling is important. Some very experienced drillers who are familiar with the automated machines can probably drill many different types of grips on their machines, but I'll take a straight drill press for my own drilling.

3 Spans and Hole Sizes

Spans

As I have said before, span is the easiest measurement to obtain with accuracy. Usually, however, drillers will fit the bowler with excessively wide spans for one or both fingers. A very simple check for correctness of span can be made. This is to insert the fingers into the holes until the inner bend at the appropriate knuckles (the first for a fingertip grip; the second for a conventional) aligns exactly with the leading edges of the holes. Then, the thumb should drop freely into the thumbhole. The thumb should not be hindered by touching either the leading edge of the hole or the back of the hole before it is almost fully inserted. One should expect a clean release from appropriate span and pitch. Further, with the offset thumbhole, one should not have to turn or rotate the inserted fingers to position the thumb for insertion. This movement is often necessary with the standard centerline thumbhole grip even though identical measured spans are drilled.

In the fingertip grip, the appropriate spans for each finger will result in the same feel or pressure on each finger during the swing. This indicates that each finger is sharing the load equally. The fingers will not lie flat on the surface of the ball; they will bend or arch at the second joint. This arch is necessary to position the first joints for effective lift at the release — i. e. the use of forward pitch in the fingerholes. Flattening of the fingers onto the ball surface indicates excessive span (sometimes called a "stretch" fingertip grip), the first joints or pads of the fingertips would be positioned so that reverse pitch (away from the thumb) of the fingerholes would be necessary to align the holes with the angle of the fingertips. The pitch reversal is necessary to accommodate the lack of bend of the fingers, and such a reversal can result in loss of the ball (slippage) off the fingers during

35

the swing or in a premature release. As you can gather, *I do not believe in a stretch or relaxed fingertip grip — there is only one appropriate fingertip grip for a particular hand. Individual hand flexibility may allow for variance in spans, but not to the extent that the stretch or relaxed fingertip concepts require.*

(***Author's Note:*** Today, it is more common to see insufficient span in fingertip grips. Drillers claim that they are fitting a "relaxed" fingertip grip, but it is actually underspanned. Again, this error may be caused by insufficiently stretching the hand over the fitting device. There is really no rationale for this grip.)

Figure 9: The Correct Spans for a Fingertip Grip

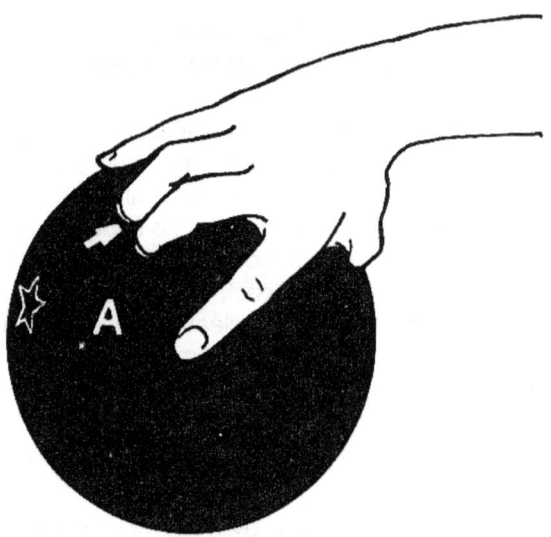

Figure 9 shows how the proper spans appear. Notice the similar appearance of both fingers indicating the even distribution of load on each pad. Note the emergence of the fingers; one cannot see the fingernails. The bend of the knuckle is approximately 1/8" to 3/16" above the ball surface. The span would be too narrow if the bend were aligned with the ball surface and/or if the flesh between the first and second joints were allowed to enter the holes. I always tell my customers that the spans are correct if one could take a playing card, slide it toward the fingers along the surface of the ball (in the direction of the arrow at A, Figure 9), and observe that it contacts the knuckle at the point where the skin is thinnest — i. e. the bony part of the knuckle.

For a conventional grip, the same basic criteria apply. Each finger should share equally the load. The second knuckle should not contact the far edge of the hole (narrow span), and the span should not seem to stretch the joint in any way. The fingers emerge from the holes approximately 1/2' to 5/8" at the bend, and the fingers are inserted into the holes parallel with the angle of the pitch. In this way, distribution of the load will be equal along the entire length of the first and second joints.

Since there is no reliable criterion for determining semifingertip spans, I will not recommend use of this grip. Span, as well as the flexibility of the finger at the second joint, roughly determines the pitches to be used, so this grip is highly individual to the user. Likewise, it is a very difficult task to copy the feel of this ball into another ball.

Round holes are drilled, but these should be smaller than required to admit the finger or thumb. This starting or beginning hole should then be carefully shaped to approximate the shape requirements of the finger or thumb. I recommend the following simple criteria for choosing starting hole sizes to be drilled.

Hole Sizes

(**Author's Note:** This discussion does not consider the use of modern-day finger and thumb inserts.)

Almost without exception, bowlers are using excessively large finger and thumb holes. Even when the spans are appropriate, the holes are often too large. The reasons for this are rather simple. One, the drilling machine can drill only round holes, and the hole is fitted loosely to accommodate only the widest part of the finger. Second, even though correctly-sized starting holes may be drilled, the fit may be disfigured by the bevel or rotary sander. I will discuss this instrument of destruction in more detail in the chapter devoted to the fitting process.)

Any thumbhole: Fit the bowler with a hole size that admits the thumb with some resistance. This hole should be large enough to admit the thumb without pain but it should resist the thumb slightly from turning (rotating) within the hole.

(***Author's Note:*** Because the thumb usually does rotate in the hole during the release, the thumbhole should be enlarged appropriately to allow for some rotation.)

Fingertip fingerholes: The holes should be large enough to admit the fingers until they stop gently with the inner crease of the first joint 1/8" from the leading edge of the holes. The middle fingerhole should feel the same size to its finger as the ring fingerhole does to the ring finger.

Conventional fingerholes: The holes should be large enough to admit the fingers until they stop slightly before the second knuckle is reached. The top 1/4" of the inner surface of the holes should gently contact the flesh all of the way around the fingers. This sizing will allow for slight sanding and shaping.

Working out or tooling of these starting holes is the only way to ensure a comfortable, secure fit. Only if one has almost perfectly cylindrical fingers (and I have a good friend who does) can he get a proper fit with round holes. The drilling machine cannot accomplish the fitting, and the use of the bevel sander is counterproductive. Ideally, the bowler should finish the holes himself. If he does not want to take on this responsibility, he then has every right to expect that the driller will take time and exercise extreme care in fitting his ball.

4 The Pitches

Pitch refers to the degree to which the axis of a hole is directed toward or away from the geometric center of the ball. If the axis of a hole passes directly through the geometric center of the ball, the hole is said to have zero pitch. To keep our discussion as simple as possible, let us clarify some terminology that has already been used to some extent in previous chapters. (I must apologize for having to use information that has not, to this point, been explained, but I found it necessary. When possible, I referred the reader to this chapter for definitions and for the clockface terminology. Remember what I said about circular discussions? It really is impossible to describe something without drawing from other concepts that may not have been described.) Let's pretend that the bowling balls shown in Figure 10 are clear plastic and that they will allow us to see a little over halfway through them. A dot will represent the exact geometric center of the ball (as distinct from the weight center). I have used a clockface reference system to show these balls from different perspectives. Explaining points of pitch without resorting to terms such as right and left and top and bottom is difficult. These terms have no meaning unless one assumes a particular perspective of the ball being discussed. The grips are shown for a right-handed bowler and are turned to show different perspectives indicated by the clockface numbers. For example, in diagram C the thumb is shown toward the left half of the ball as it appears to the reader. As is generally accepted, the left side of the ball for a right-handed bowler is at 9 o'clock on the printed page (perspective A) but is really at 3 o'clock as the ball rolls toward the pins. You can see the confusion that has resulted from interchanging terms.

Figure 10: .Different Perspectives of a Bowling Ball Using a Clockface Reference System

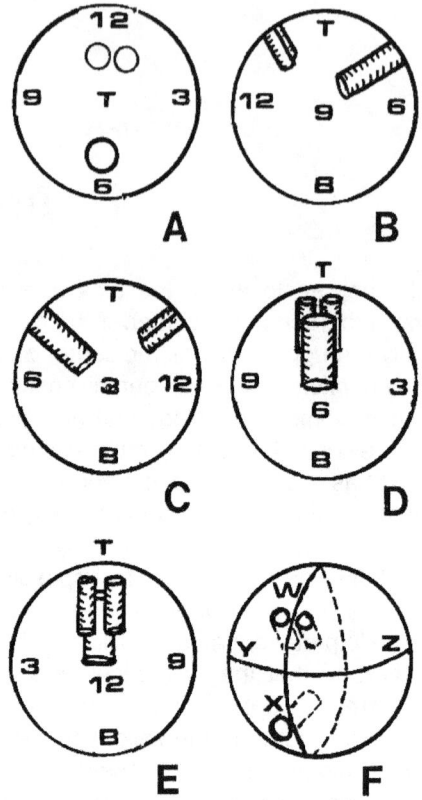

Therefore, in every case, the terms top (T) and bottom (B) will refer to that area where the label normally is placed and to that area directly through the center and on the other side of the ball, respectively. Likewise, the terms right and left will not be used unless related to the clockface system beforehand. Sometimes I will speak of lines and planes. This usually will refer to imaginary lines such as WX and YZ, which create planes that divide the ball into segments. In diagram F, the planes are shown. Line WX is the beginning grip layout line or centerline (CL). *Lines are two-dimensional while planes are three-dimensional. Lines are on the surface of an object under consideration while planes penetrate or cut through the object.*

Figure 11 shows that reverse pitch (R) is the opposite of forward (F) pitch. Unfortunately, some confusion in these terms has resulted because of the use of alternate terms such as away and toward that are usually used to refer to lateral pitch! Looking at Figure 10, we see that reverse thumbhole pitch is in the direction of 6 while reverse pitch for the fingerholes is in the direction of 12.

Figure 11: Reverse pitch (R) is the opposite of forward pitch (F). The directions of reference for thumb and finger forward/reverse pitch are 180 degrees different.

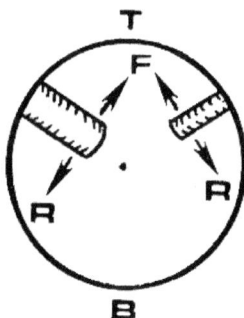

To keep these terms straight, remember two points. The first is that forward and reverse pitches refer to pitches of the fingerholes and the thumbhole along the wrist-to-finger tip axis only. The second is that forward pitch means that the hole is drilled away from the geometric center of the ball toward the other hole or set of holes. Reverse pitch means the hole is drilled away from the geometric center of the ball and in a direction further away from the other hole or set of holes.

Presently, there appear, at least in the literature, to be two schools of thought in the reference points of pitch relative to the geometric center of the ball. Say, for example, we drill 1" reverse pitch in a single hole.

Figure 12: Reference Points of Pitch

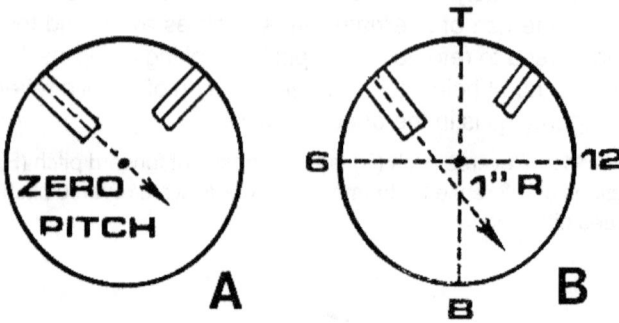

As shown in Figure 12, we may say that this inch is the distance of deviation of the axis of that hole behind (plane 6-12) or below (plane T-B) the geometric center. Some drilling machines are designed to select pitch in either or both ways. The difference should not be significant since the distance along either plane should be 1". The second type of pitch lies on a plane perpendicular to that of forward/reverse pitch, and roughly aligns with the width of the hand.

Figure 13: Pitch Terminology for a Right-handed Grip – A. Directions of forward (F) and reverse (R) pitch. B. Directions or right lateral (RL) and left lateral (LL) pitch.

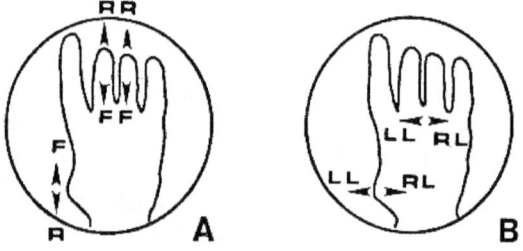

Figure 13 shows a comparison and introduces lateral pitch. The terms right and left lateral pitch are also used when referring to left-handed bowlers but the meanings are reversed. That is, left lateral thumb pitch for a left-handed bowler is directed to a greater degree (than zero pitch) under the palm while right lateral thumb pitch for a right-handed bowler is directed to a greater degree under the palm. The terms palm and away pitch seem to be falling into disuse because they are meaningless when describing lateral pitch of the fingerholes.

Right and left are more descriptive and can apply to both finger and thumb holes, but they still take on opposite meanings when comparing right and left-handed grips. Therefore, I would like to propose the terms ablateral and adlateral to better standardize the terms describing lateral pitches. Since the prefixes ab- and ad- mean toward and away from the thumb side of the hand, respectively, the terms would apply to both left and right-handed bowlers in the same way. Figure 14 shows how these terms would apply to right and left-handed grips.

Figure 14: Lateral Pitch Terminology
LL= left lateral, RL = right lateral, AB = ablateral, AD = adiateral

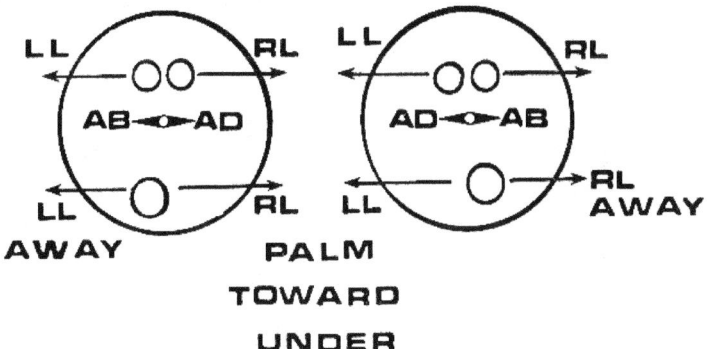

Remember that ablateral pitches will always be toward the thumb side of the hand while adlateral pitches will be away from the thumb side of the hand regardless of the handedness of the bowler. (Incidentally, it is the abductor set of finger muscles that take the strain of the lift and turn of the release.)

Obviously, any amount of pitch may be drilled into the holes, the reasonable limitation being the possibility of running the fingerholes together at the bottom. Pitches must be chosen carefully, but in practice, they are left to the discretion of the driller who can and does make arbitrary judgements. He often will recommend pitches that he uses himself.

I suggest that pitches should be based on the relative orientation of the fingers that gives the most effortlessly powerful grip. The planes of pitch (resulting from the combination of forward/reverse and lateral pitch for each hole) should be parallel with the direction of flex of the fingers. (The thumb pitches must be a compromise of the direction of flex and the direction of the grip, but this will be explained later.) This requires a minimum of four and a maximum of six planes of pitch (two for each hole) for the grip. A standard drilling provides for only two planes of pitch for the entire grip.

Figure 15:
A. The direction of flex (DF) of the middle finger is parallel with the grip layout centerline (CL).
B. Label View: On the surface of the ball, the centers of the middle fingerhole and the thumbhole lie on the same line (MT).
C. Bottom View: The angle of pitch of the middle fingerhole should be parallel with the centerline plane.
D. 6 O'Clock View: Showing parallelism of MH and CL planes
E. 6 O'Clock View: The thumbhole pitch plane (TH) intersects plane CL

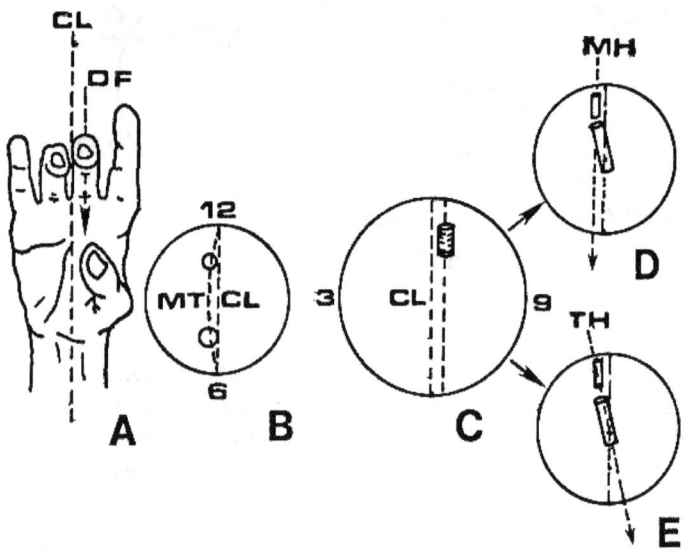

Middle Fingerhole Pitch

As indicated by Figure 15, the middle finger tends to flex toward the inner part of the base of the thumb. This suggests a parallel relationship between the forward/reverse pitch and the centerline plane of the grip. Drilling the hole should reflect this tendency. The proper way to envision the pitch relationship between the middle fingerhole and the thumbhole is shown in Figure 15. Even if the middle fingerhole has zero forward/reverse pitch, the lateral pitch will not be zero (see the chapter on drilling for details).

The amount of forward/reverse pitch in the middle fingerhole is determined by the span between it and the thumbhole. *The objective at the explosion point of the release is to have the entire pad of the finger tip in contact with the entire gripping surface of the hole at the instant the thumb clears the thumbhole.* Trial and error is necessary to determine this pitch, but a general rule is that, during the swing, the pressure near the joint should be greater than the pressure near the tip (the same does not hold true for a conventional). Obviously, excessively wide span does not allow for the desired use of the pitches in the fingerholes. A sufficient amount of the finger tips must be in the holes for the maximum benefit of pitch to be obtained.

Ring Fingerhole Pitch

As shown in Figure 16, the ring finger probably will tend to flex toward the thumb also. However, this is not always the case with all hands.

Figure 16: Ring Fingerhole Pitch – The direction of flex of the ring finger (DF) is not usually parallel with the grip layout centerline plane (CL). It may intersect this plane because of individual hand characteristics and because of the conformity of the hand to the ball surface (ARC).

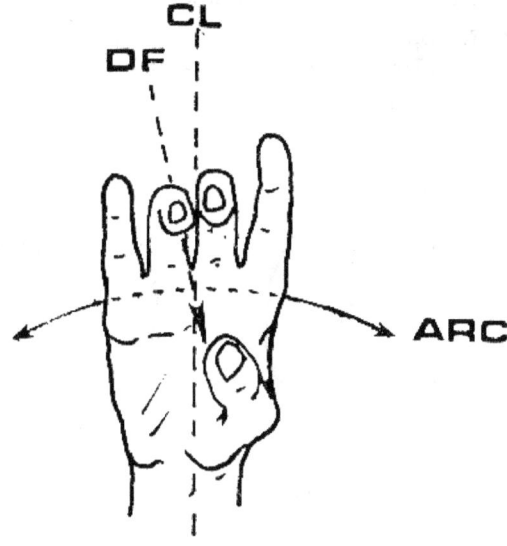

Often, the ring finger will point away from the thumb or in a manner parallel with the middle finger. My suggestion for accommodating the ring finger is to determine the direction of flex relative to the thumb, mark it on the ball on the grip layout, and drill forward/reverse pitch parallel with that direction. In this method, lateral pitch would be set on zero (see the chapter on drilling), and the amount of forward/reverse pitch would still be determined by the span between thumb and ring fingerholes. This method may not be advisable for conventional grips or wider grips with large, deep fingerholes because the possibility of running the holes together at the bottom is increased. As in the case of the middle fingerhole, the pressure of the pitch during the swing should be nearer the joint, and this almost invariably means that forward pitch will be chosen for both holes to achieve this feel. An exception would be for extremely wide spans.

Relating Middle Fingerhole Pitch to Ring Fingerhole Pitch

Since span determines the proper forward/reverse pitch and since the spans are usually different from each other, one can expect that the pitches will be different also. For the same feel of pitch with the proper spans, there will usually be less forward pitch in the ring fingerhole than in the middle fingerhole.

Figure 17: Options of Pitch Based Upon a Different Starting Position For the Top of the Thumbhole – In both cases A and B, the thumbhole axis would pass through the geometric center of the ball if zero pitch were chosen.

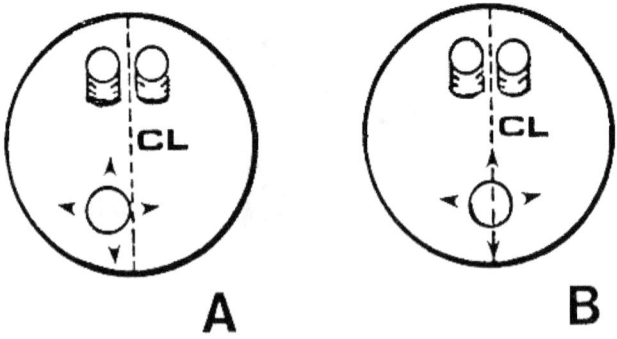

A   B

Thumbhole Pitch

This is the most important pitch involved in the grip in terms of security during the swing and release and in terms of changing the effects of roll. I feel that the offset thumbhole grip is the only one that takes into account the position of comfort and strength of the thumb. The selection of pitches relative to the positioning of the thumbhole in the grip layout cannot be overemphasized. Consider Figure 17, which shows pitch options based on the two different starting positions for the top of the thumbhole (in each case the axis of the hole would begin at zero pitch). Grip A is the offset thumbhole drilling, and grip B is the standard drilling. You can see that any pitch selected for the thumbhole of ball B is based on the notion that the thumb is in the center of the palm and that the fingers flex in directions on either side of the thumb. This idea is ridiculous!

Lateral thumbhole pitches based on a centerline starting position of the thumbhole promote crowding of the large muscle mass at the base near the palm. Most thumbs cannot move laterally in a perfectly perpendicular direction to the centerline anyway, and attempting to start changing pitches with the thumbhole superimposed on the centerline just complicates matters. The hollow of the hand formed when the grip is made is larger with the centerline thumbhole because of this crowding, hence the need for devices such as a padded glove that attempts to fill this hollow space. The main selling point of these devices is to give a cleaner, faster release. Why should one not get the best release without the aid of a device? Note that in grip B, pitch selection is based on a more correct starting position for the thumbhole.

Relating Thumbhole Pitch to the Action of the Thumb

Hold your hand in a simulated bowling grip with the palm toward you. As the thumb is moved toward and away from the index finger (thumb tip toward your face as you look at your palm) in a direction parallel with the finger tip-to-elbow plane, it is evident that the thumb rotates slightly. This rotation implies that, as the forward/reverse pitch of the thumbhole is changed, the lateral pitch must be changed in accordance to maintain the pressure of the grip on basically the same gripping surface of the thumb. Observe Figure 18, which indicates the difference between the direction of flex of the fingers and thumb (DF) and the direction of the span (DS).

Figure 18: A Comparison of the Directions of Flex of the Fingers and Thumb (DF) and the Direction of the Span (DS)

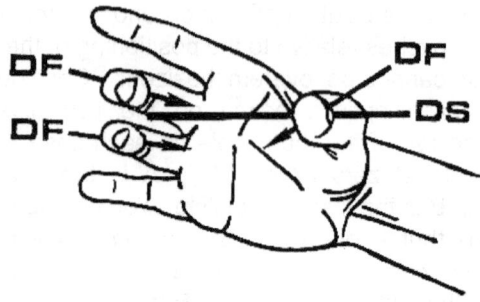

As the thumb moves toward the index finger (more forward pitch), the rotation moves the gripping face of the thumb toward the side closest to the index finger. As more reverse pitch is effected, the gripping face moves more toward the thumb pad (that has its center in the direction of flex). *At no time does the gripping face coincide with the ideal area of the thumb — the center of the pad.* The point is that; in the case of the thumbhole; pitch, size, and contour of the hole must result in a compromise between the flexing face (pad) and gripping face (off-center toward the side) so that maximum distribution of pressure over a larger area of the thumb results. The direction of flex of the thumb does not change much with differences in forward/reverse pitch but the gripping face does turn. This is one reason that changing thumb pitches can promote formation of callouses in new areas. One may choose more adlateral pitch (Figure 14) in an attempt to move the gripping face more toward the pad center, but the gripping face will remain to the side of the thumb because of the direction of the span (Figure 18). The only way to ensure even distribution of the pressure of the grip on the exact center of the pad of the thumb would be to have a hand in which the thumb is located in the exact center of the palm. Of course, the thumb would have to flex in the direction of the bridge, and I know of no one who has this type of hand.

The proper combination of forward/reverse and lateral pitch gives maximum distribution of the grip pressure over the widest area of the gripping surface possible. The release can be clean and the grip secure because the work is distributed more evenly on the thumb, and at the release point, the gripping area can release the grip surface of the inside of the hole at one time (no drag at any one place), instantaneously.

Forward/Reverse Thumbhole Pitch

There is no hard, fast rule concerning the amount of reverse pitch to use in the thumbhole. Common sense should dictate that too much reverse pitch would allow for dropping the ball and that too much forward pitch would shift the gripping surface onto the side of the thumb and hence promote drag at the release. Since the thumb is not involved in lift directly, pitch cannot be chosen in the same way that forward/reverse pitch is chosen for fingerholes (i.e. by the span). I personally use 5/8" reverse pitch in a rubber ball, but this may be excessive for some people.

(**Author's Note:** Coinciding with the use of plastic balls and thumb slugs, I reduced the amount of reverse thumb pitch to 1/4" — appropriate for my 4 5/8" middle fingerhole span.)

Bill Taylor recommends the selection of reverse thumbhole pitch based on release requirements (that he has observed but not explained) and on the length of span. He draws a line through the ball from the inner (leading) edges of the thumbhole and middle fingerhole. The angle formed by this straight line and the gripping surface of the thumbhole, he states, should be 63 degrees. He terms this the optimum release angle, and I refer you to his book, ***How to Fit and Drill a Bowling Ball*** for a chart that gives the amount of reverse pitch necessary to maintain this 63-degree release angle with various spans. I do not know how helpful this release angle can be; it tends to give much less reverse pitch than most users of wide spans are accustomed to, but Taylor's idea deserves a try. (Remember, however, that Taylor bases his entire concept of pitch on a standard drilling with a centerline-positioned thumbhole.) The old Ebonite drilling manual recommended 1/8" forward pitch for spans less than 3-1/4"; zero pitch for spans between 3-1/4" and 3-3/4"; 1/8" reverse pitch for spans from 3-3/4" to 4-1/4"; and 1/4" reverse pitch for spans over 4-1/4". This was the convention used for many years, and I am certain that other manuals convey other ideas as to the best or recommended pitches. Also, since no one has a really dependable formula for determining thumbhole pitch, there is, of course, no good instrument to measure it. I have no constructive comments to add at this writing concerning this measurement. One important thing to remember is that *what feels comfortable in a grip while the ball rests on the table or during a few practice swings is not necessarily what is best in a grip for consistently good bowling.* One must use various combinations of pitch for a period of time to draw valid conclusions as to their effectiveness.

Lateral Thumbhole Pitch

A general rule is that more adlateral (under the palm) pitch is used when the bowler wants more turn on the ball at the release (with resultant lowering of the track). Ablateral (away from the palm) pitch gives a faster release and consequently does not allow the thumb to stay in the ball long enough for the bowler to turn the ball to any great extent. It has been my experience that ablateral pitch is not useful with the offset thumbhole grip that gives a faster release anyway.

(**Author's Note:** For persons with limited range of motion of the thumb base joint, ablateral pitch is often needed to bring the gripping surface of the thumbhole to meet as much of the thumb gripping surface as possible. In this case, the bowler may have to use a lighter-weight ball. Further, most drillers usually give the bowler too much adlateral pitch for comfort. The less reverse pitch, the more uncomfortable any lateral pitch seems. (See Figure 14 and demonstrate these effects to yourself.)

Measurement of lateral pitch is a problem also. Most drillers use the estimation system originated by Bill Bunetta. This amounts to having the customer grab a pencil with the bowling finger and thumb tips and observing the direction that the thumb points relative to the position of the fingers. The same test is conducted by having the customer clasp his or the driller's wrist and noting the thumb position in the same way. Bill Taylor uses essentially the same system, but he has attempted to quantify the pitch values. He has a bowler grasp a piece of pipe upon which a scale has been affixed. This scale shows the pitches in 1/8" increments.

Both methods are, at best, estimations and leave much to be desired. There needs to be developed a better method of measurement that takes into account both the direction of flex of the thumb and the direction of the spans. I regret that, at this time, I can offer no improvement to their systems. Some drillers are skilled, and their experience compensates for deficiencies in measurement, so do not be afraid to work with a driller and experiment to find the best pitch requirement for you. I feel that you will find that any more than 1/4" of adlateral pitch will not be useful and will tend to promote overturning of the ball to eliminate drag during the release, but this must be determined individually. **With the offset thumbhole, the pitches will measure true, but zero lateral pitch will feel that it is slightly adlateral due to the position of the top of the thumbhole relative to the positions and pitches of the fingerholes.**

One Last Word Concerning Pitch

The feel of pitch and sometimes the actual measurement will be influenced greatly by the amount of bevel and contour of the hole. Too much bevel will narrow spans and therefore appear to create more reverse pitch than desired. It is for this reason that it is absolutely essential to fit correct spans and to use moderate bevel to ensure measurements close to those predicted.

5 The Release

Leverage – The Efficient Use of Energy

The central theme of this discussion is the role of leverage in the delivery. Leverage is the characteristic that allows a small man to lift heavier objects than expected or to hit a golf ball a long distance down the fairway. In the case of the golfer, the feet are planted firmly, and the perfection of his timing results in the transfer of most of the energy from his feet, through the legs and trunk, down through the arms and club shaft, and finally to the club face that comes in contact with the ball. All parts of the body, however, must be in the proper position at any instant during the swing for maximum transference of this energy to the ball. This is kinesiologically correct and gives maximum leverage that results in optimum power and control.

Although the bowler is in motion during his swing, his body must be in the proper position at the foul line for optimum transfer of energy from the feet to the fingers. If you remember, I said earlier that the bowling delivery is actually a system of interconnected parts each of which must be functioning properly if the system is to function properly. Many well-known instructors have analyzed this system in terms of parallel and perpendicular lines. Three of them, Lou Bellisimo of Oregon, and Les Barrett (my former coach) and Bill Taylor of California, have worked hard to perfect their teaching methods, and I would recommend sessions with these gentlemen (or any other fine instructor that I have unintentionally omitted) to improve your game. If you cannot get personal instruction, there are several books that can help you, and these are listed in the section titled, "Recommended Reading."

For our purposes, I will list what I feel are only some of the important characteristics of the delivery. Then, I will concentrate my attention on the hand and arm and how the bowling grip relates to them during the swing and release. This relationship has never been properly explained in terms of the fit of the ball, and I will develop this subject in detail. Finally, I will relate the grip, hand, arm, and the swing to the entire approach and delivery in an attempt to explain how the proper or improper fit of the grip strongly influences the effectiveness of the entire delivery.

Some Important Elements of the Delivery

The following are some of the important elements of the approach and delivery. Please refer to some of the books listed in the section "Recommended Reading" for fundamental details.

1. **The Stance (Setup)**: This position is extremely important because the maintenance of proper balance during the entire delivery begins here. The start of the approach can be thought of as giving a hula hoop a push across a gymnasium floor. If you take time to line up the hoop and push it perfectly in the center of the tracking area, the hoop will travel unhindered until it falls over some distance from the point of origin. However, if you neglect to start the hoop perpendicular to the floor and/or if you give it an off-center push, the hoop will wobble, veer off to one side, and fall over a shorter distance from the original starting point. This is not to say that you will wobble and fall over if you are not well-balanced during your bowling stance, but it does imply that imbalance during the stance can more subtly interfere with the delivery than can be realized by the bowler. The better the start, the better the chances for proper balance at the foul line.

2. **The Steps (Footwork)**: No matter how many steps in the delivery, the objective is the orderly transference of weight from one foot to the other so that optimum balance will be maintained throughout the approach. Spotty (sticky or slippery) approaches are the primary cause of bowling badly. Their influence is even stronger than that of the lane because proper transfer of weight from one foot to another is made impossible. Likewise, the steps are made inconsistently from one delivery to another. This inconsistency makes us consciously control the muscles because extra care must be taken in each step so as to maintain balance. This controlled

action makes for more tension in the delivery, and this is an undesirable characteristic. However, it is the only way to insure some sort of control on inferior approaches. The entire delivery, not just the steps, is a subconscious effort overridden by the conscious mind that concentrates on the target. The mind trusts the body to do the correct thing during the delivery, but this trust is impossible when lane and approach conditions are inconsistent. If proper balance can be maintained or preserved from the beginning of the approach, the body should be in the proper position for maximum leverage at the release.

3. *The Swing*: The swing should be as effortlessly powerful as possible (see chapter 1). The essential characteristic of the swing is that it should be perfectly circular. If a high-speed photographic analysis of the swing is done, one can see that a well-balanced approach should bring about a perfectly circular swing and followthrough. Further, the followthrough should be the same speed as the downswing.

4. *The Slide (Finish)*: The slide should be perfectly parallel with the direction of the ball toward the target. It should not necessarily be perpendicular to the foul line. More than any other facet of the approach and delivery, the slide allows the greatest degree of correction for slight imperfections in timing. During the slide, there is time to correct for a slightly misdirected or mistimed swing. It is undesirable to have to use this correction step but it happens unconsciously to good bowlers simply because no one can deliver the ball in exactly the same way for every delivery. (Important: see Subconscious Correction in the glossary).

(*Author's Note:* Today, many are striving for a "flat swing." In doing so, they often lean over, bend the elbow, or use some sort of wrist action to push the ball through the release. Actually, none of these movements are necessary, because the flatness of the swing is controlled by the length of the slide, the axis of the swing being moved forward horizontally. The longer the slide, the flatter the swing during the downswing and release. The long slide accomplishes the flat swing more consistently than any of the other movements.)

In *The Secret of Bowling Strikes*, Dawson Taylor explained the squeeze (flex) of the fingers at the explosion point. This explosion point terminology is very colorful but, unfortunately, sometimes misleading. Nothing abrupt or catastrophic should happen at the release point of the ball, and this is really what Taylor explained. For maximum leverage, the entire body must be in the proper position. The release, if certain muscle strengthening exercises have been practiced (remember the development of muscle balance), will be more powerful because the entire potential energy of each facet of the delivery comes into play at the exact instant of the release point. A great amount of energy is transferred from the feet to the fingers at this point, and the grip must be fitted properly for this energy transfer to be maximized without strain on the hand. The release can be envisioned as withdrawing savings from a bank account. Deposits have been made at intervals (the steps) and the entire amount can be withdrawn (the release) at one time. This is called the "summation of internal forces" along a "kinetic chain."

Relationship of Foul Line Body Position to Leverage

Let's perform a brief plane analysis of the body position at the foul line. Figure 19 shows the author simulating the release point in the delivery. Two views are presented.

Figure 19: A Plane Analysis of the Body Position at the Foul Line

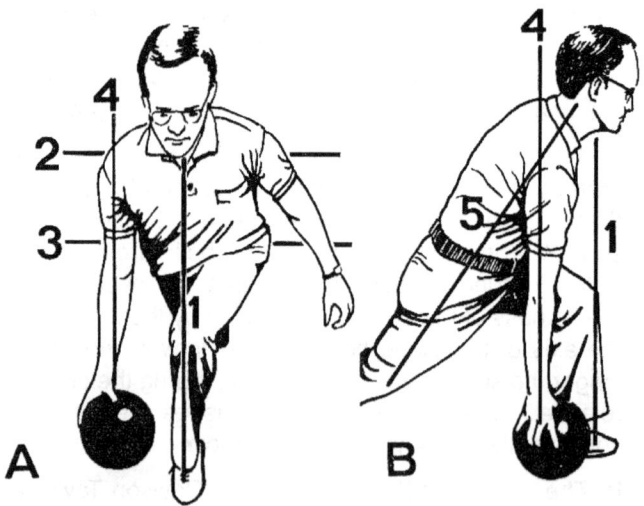

Notice that, for achieving proper balance at the foul line, plane 1 is important. As picture A shows, the chin is aligned with the left knee and the ball of the foot. Picture B shows that the alignment is also on a single plane when viewed from the side. Plane 2 should be roughly parallel with the approach but not with the foul line unless the target line is perpendicular to the foul line. One should strive keep this plane parallel even though the weight of the ball tends to pull it down. It should always be parallel with plane 3, which runs through the hips. Plane 5 is more a result than a cause of the positions that establish plane 1. It does illustrate the angle of the body established by adherence to the chin-knee-foot alignment. Even when starting from a completely upright position, *when the ball goes into the downswing from the extended pushaway, the body will have a 20-degree forward orientation of the trunk during the approach.* This position should be maintained through the release, with no additional forward bend at the waist.

The energy transfer link between the shoulders and the fingers is illustrated by plane 4. This shows the importance of a perfectly straight relationship from the pivot point of the arm at the shoulder to the pads of the fingers. This plane should be parallel with plane 1 at the point of release and perpendicular to planes 2 and 3. To clarify what I have just said and to start you on your way to analysis of your own delivery, ask yourself, "What happens when any of these planes are misaligned?" Study Figure 19 for a time and try to predict what happens to the ball path in relation to the target line when the planes misalign. Finally, memorize the planes that I have just discussed (not necessarily the numbers) and use them each time you practice.

Relationship of the Grip to Leverage

Having assumed that the duration of the average delivery is two seconds and that the length between the pivot point of the shoulder and the center of the ball is 26 inches, I used a physics formula to get a rough idea of how much a 16-pound ball really weighs at the release. I obtained a reasonable estimate of 22 pounds (see the end of this chapter for details of this formula). It is apparent that, for maximum energy transfer with minimum effort, this 22 pounds must be distributed evenly on the pad surfaces of both fingertips. How can this be accomplished? By the parallel alignment of the long plane of the arm (plane 4, Figure 19) with the original layout centerline of the grip. Since this line divides the ball into halves with a fingerhole on either side, the distribution of the weight will fall equally on either side of the plane with each finger taking an equal share of the load.

Naturally, since the thumb is not in the middle of the palm, the thumbhole must be offset to allow for ease of alignment of the grip centerline and plane 4. Figure 20 shows a comparison of the offset thumbhole grip and the standard grip and their alignment with the long plane of the arm. With the standard grip, in order for the thumb to be comfortable, the ball will slightly adduct the hand at the wrist (see Figure 1).

(*Authors Note:* The ring fingerhole span is usually greater than the middle fingerhole span. Therefore, with a standard grip, the ball tends to rotate forward during the downswing to distribute the load evenly on both fingers and alleviate rubbing of the top of the thumbhole on the thumb. This rotation occurs regardless of pitch; it is more a function of the difference in spans, but it is made more severe by the gripping action of the fingers. This effect can be minimized by offsetting the thumbhole and establishing the pitch relationships explained below.)

Figure 20: Alignment of the Grip Layout Centerline (CL) with the Long Plane of the Arm (P4) in the Offset Thumbhole Grip (A) and in the Standard Grip (B)

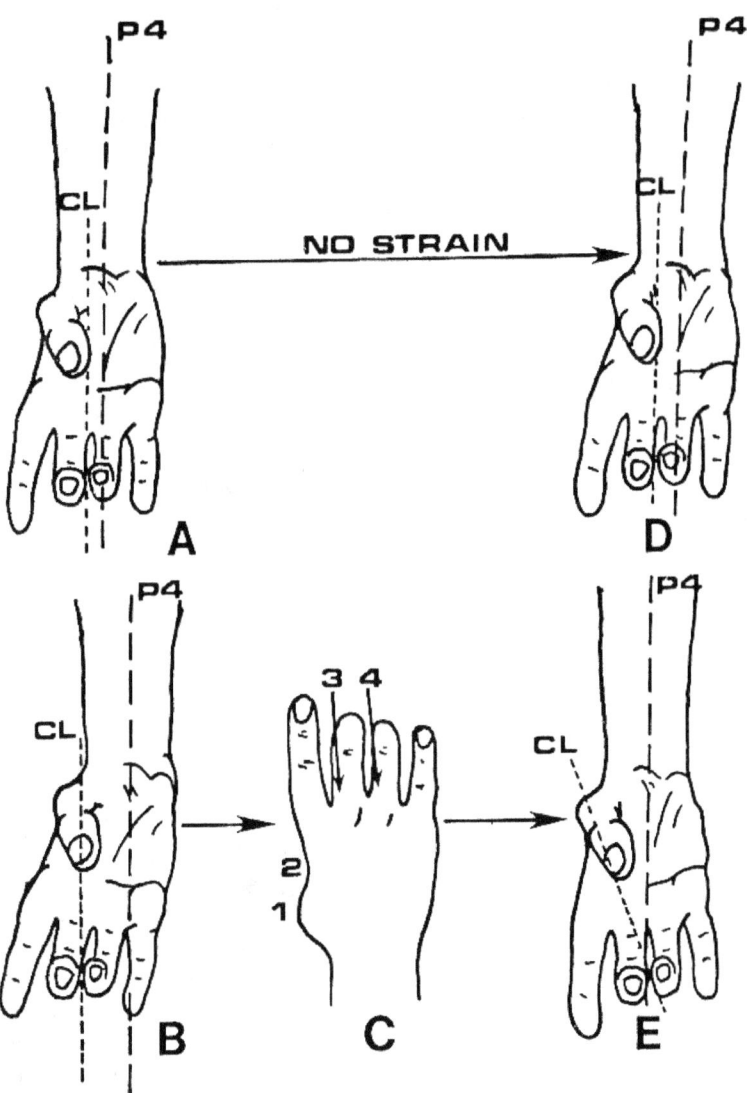

This motion, in response to several points of stress on the hand, attempts to align the centerline and plane 4 with a standard drilling. This alignment of which I speak is simply another way of saying that the most important wrist position in bowling is not flexion-extension. Rather, it is the abduction-adduction position. If these two planes are aligned, the wrist should be in the 180-degree position with respect to abduction-adduction. *At no time should the wrist be forced to be adducted, but the standard grip promotes adduction of the wrist!*

(*Author's Note:* Because modern balls on synthetic lanes often hook immediately upon touchdown, it is often necessary to adduct the wrist to apply more "spin" to the ball at the release, hence delaying the break. However, it is still preferable not to adduct the wrist to ensure less effort in producing good leverage)

Looking at Figure 20 more closely, we notice that drawings A and D depict the offset grip and that drawings B, C, and D depict the standard grip. With the offset thumbhole, the hand has no trouble keeping the centerline aligned with the long plane of the arm (P4), even when the wrist is in the 180-degree extended position. Assuming that time is passing during the swing from drawing A to drawing D, we see that no strain is put upon the hand while holding the ball. The planes will remain aligned comfortably, and good leverage will result at the release with maximum energy transfer from the shoulder to the fingers.

In the case of the standard grip with the thumbhole superimposed on the centerline, alignment of the centerline with the long plane of the arm may be quite impossible for some people. The hand, as shown in B, must be abducted to a great extent (and the wrist may be cupped) to effect alignment. Diagram C shows the points of strain or stress resulting from maintaining the position shown in diagram B. The edge of the thumbhole rubs against the bone at point 1, and the muscles and tendons are stretched at point 2 (not to mention crowding of the large muscle mass of the thumb within the palm). Further the abductor muscles of the fingers (points 3 and 4) are stretched, while their opposing muscles, the adductors are not participating in sharing the load. If we assume that time passes from diagram B to diagram E, the hand will adduct to relieve the stresses of the grip in the swing, and the centerline will no longer be aligned with plane 4 at the explosion point. The energy transfer link is broken at the wrist, and maximum leverage is no longer possible at the release. Please try these movements yourself with bowling ball in hand.

What I am leading up to is the conclusion that the standard grip is inappropriate for optimum energy transfer from feet to fingers.

Truly, the spans, pitches, and hole sizes may be proper, but unless the offset thumbhole grip as I have described it is used, and further, unless the pitches are drilled as described in chapter four, the ball does not meet the requirements of the hand, swing, or the delivery! Rather, the ball fits the requirements of the drilling machine or the requirements of well-accepted but erroneous concepts of grip that are propagated by almost every driller today. I am, therefore, so strongly opposed to the thoughtless repetition of drillers of fitting every customer with the standard grip, that I have decided to include an entire chapter that gives stepwise directions in the drilling of the offset thumbhole grip. Just as important is the chapter on the actual fitting process — the contouring of the holes to achieve optimum fit.

In about 1960, All-Star champion (now ABC Hall of Fame member) Harry "Tiger" Smith recommended the use of red rubber fingerhole inserts for added leverage at the release. These "Tiger Grip" inserts never really gained popularity, probably because their use made the ball hook too early when a crisp delivery of the ball was effected. When a bowler minimized his downswing speed and lift (called "babying" or "fudging" the shot), the ball reacted more favorably on the lane. However, pins were more resistant 20 years ago, so there was some sacrifice of pin-carrying ability with the slower or softer delivery. Smith turned (horizontal rotation) the ball to a great extent at the release, and rubber inserts were probably more useful to bowlers who did the same. Over the years since then, small strips to be inserted into regular fingerholes (Ace Mitchell cork grips, Pro Grip rubber grips, etc.) have stayed on the scene, while rubber inserts that completely encircled the fingers went by the wayside. In the last few years, however, a new variable has been introduced — the extremely slick, oil-covered urethane lane finish. This has presented a new environment that favors greater lift and turn with less forward ball speed. (I will preach to you in chapter six about the less-resistant modern bowling pin.) Consequently, the use of inserts has become popular. They have brought a new dimension to bowling for me, personally, but looking at the situation objectively, they may not continue to be useful with innovative changes in lane surfaces in subsequent years. Likewise, these grips may not be helpful to everyone, but I do recommend that any bowler try a set in one soft-surfaced and one hard-surfaced ball.

The new inserts are made of soft plastic, are available at most pro shops, and are molded in various finger sizes. The outer diameter is standard, usually 1" or less (actually 31/32" or 63/64" O.D.). The original fingerholes are drilled to fit the outer diameter of the inserts (watch the spans!), which are then cemented in place (I recommend Goodyear's Pliobond over the Super Glue-type or over the black rubber adhesives. It withstands the summer heat, and the inserts can be removed and repositioned without destruction to them or to the ball.). Sufficient bridge should be left to assure stability of the inserts and so that the remaining material will not chip out. The holes should be drilled *slowly* to avoid the chatter that may be common with the larger drill sizes. These measures, along with flattening the bridge to avoid pin contact, should minimize cracking problems later.

If you need more information about the availability of either the white or the gold inserts, contact:

Pro Sports Systems, Inc.
6714 NE 18th St.
Vancouver, WA 98661

Bowling Gloves and Wrist Supports

I had originally intended to devote an entire chapter to this subject but decided against it for two reasons. First, quite frankly, such products appear on the market so fast that any review of them would be outdated before publication of this book. Secondly, I really do not know enough detail about each device to discuss them at length.

Very simply, these devices perform one or both of two functions — to fill in the hollow of the hand and to hold the wrist in a single position throughout the swing and release. The gloves have been sold to thousands of users to give them a more positive grip and a quicker release. Actually, the pad does keep the bowler from inserting the thumb too far into the hole, but it does not even contact the ball during the swing and release — only during the stance and pushaway. *It is my opinion that the padded glove was developed to compensate for the crowding of the thumb by the centerline thumbhole of the standard grip.* The crowding, as you remember, results in a larger hollow space between the palm and the ball.

The wrist supports, I feel, may prohibit the user from making essential minor modifications to the wrist position during the stance. If used constantly, they interfere with the development of muscle tone and balance because they share in part of the load that promotes working of the muscles. These supports are a blessing, however, to those with weak wrists, and they also serve a vital function in keeping the wrist from adducting. Keeping the wrist straight must be learned, and the brace or support is only a reminder or learning device — not a permanent crutch.

The Shoes — An Integral Part of Leverage

To have the best possible leverage on each and every delivery, one must be sure of his footing. He must be secure at the release point. I advise that the best shoes be purchased — ones with distinct sliding and breaking soles of different composition. Custom-made shoes are available from:

> Linds World IMPEX
> 501 Laser Drive
> Somerset, WI 54025

Inquiries involving problems with the feet or the shoes should be made directly to the company.

Formula for Determining the Weight of the Bowling Ball at the Point of Release (How Technical Can You Get?)

If you are interested in finding out the downward force of your bowling ball at the release, use the following steps.

1. Weigh your bowling ball. W = weight in pounds.

2. Measure the length of your arm from the pivot point of the shoulder to the geometric center of the ball P (pendulum) = the length in inches.

3. Accurately time the duration on only the downward portion of the swing, ending with the exact instant of the release. T = time in seconds.

4. Figure exactly what portion of a circle the measured downswing represents. Express it as a fraction without units. C = a unitless fraction.

5. Assume that the pull of gravity is 384 inches per second (32 feet per second). G = 384"/second.

6. Pi = 3.1416 and is also unitless.

7. Plug the resultant figures into the following formula to find F:

$$F = W / G \times 2 (Pi) (C/T) \times P,$$

where F = centripetal force, i. e., the force required to keep the ball from flying off of the hand during the swing. It is the opposite of centrifugal force, and it is expressed in pounds, since all other units should cancel out.

8. Add F to the weight of the ball to obtain the total downward force of the ball at the instant of the release. This total force pulls directly away from the shoulder along plane P4, Figure 19.

After studying this formula, it is rather easy to explain three other factors. Notice that F is decreased when C is smaller. C, of course, is smaller with the lower backswing; hence, a lesser amount of lift is obtained. Alternatively, if T is smaller, F is greater, the logic being that a faster downswing take less time and gives more lift. A greater value for P indicates a longer arm, a greater F, and a greater lift potential.

6 Bowling Geometrics

Introduction

Think about how many times you have done the following. You arrive at the bowling center with your equipment in hand, go to your assigned lane, put your ball on the ball return, and put on your shoes. Now, the next obvious activity is to roll a few practice balls to loosen up the old muscles. It is at this point that you should make a critical decision pertaining to your bowling game. You can either waste a lot of time in your league or practice session by passively rolling the ball, or you can take a few minutes to figure out how you are going to reach the pocket with the initial delivery of each and every frame. This chapter, as well as chapter nine, will show you how to accomplish this goal. Do not pass up this opportunity!

In my travels over the last few years, I have had the pleasure to have known hundreds of very fine bowlers, many of whom average over 200 in league and tournament play. However, even taking all of their accomplishments into account, many of these bowlers do not appear to be as well-rounded as their averages would imply. In short, they do not commonly use some reliable way of aiming or lining up for their deliveries. I feel that they could be even more versatile on various lane conditions if they were to use some logical targeting system. In fact, when young bowlers begin to compete in more serious competition, they are usually taken aside and instructed in proper alignment by a seasoned professional who learned it in much the same way when he was a rookie. In this chapter, I am going to detail more of the "nuts and bolts" of the bowling game. This is called parallel line bowling (half of the process of playing lanes; the other half is adaptation to various lane conditions), and, as you will see, it really involves a rather simple system of dots, arrows, and parallel lines, similar to those commonly used in billiards. My discussion may become rather involved, but the material is not really complicated if you will follow the sequence of presentation in an orderly way. I promise to resolve the entire theme as the chapter progresses, and what you will have is a simple set of data in the form of adjusted stance positions for various trajectories (*target lines*) that are unique and tailor-made to you. You can put these to use whenever and wherever you choose to bowl. Since this chapter is devoted to the body, the swing, the approach, the lane, and the pins, and to the geometric interrelationships among them, I have chosen to call this chapter, "Bowling Geometrics."

In all fairness, I must say that there have been a few rather useful explanations of playing lanes in previous texts. One, **Add 30 Pins to your Bowling Score** by Billy Welu, contained a chapter devoted to parallel line bowling. This is a book for beginners, however, and I suppose that Billy was correct in explaining things in a do-as-I-say manner for the sake of simplicity. Explanations of the different aiming systems are presented in an overview fashion but are not critically examined. The book is exceptionally good, however, and I suggest that it be made a part of every bowler's holdings.

Because I feel that there is no true distinction between spot and line bowling, I will present my opinions about line bowling in a very different manner. Further, since I want you to have a good grasp of a system that you can begin to use as soon as you have completed this chapter, and in keeping with the fundamental philosophy of this book, I will provide you with elements of a framework upon which you yourself can build from your own bowling experience. Besides, I hope to tell you things that you just may not have thought about! Before we get a running start, let me answer a possible criticism of this chapter. Some persons may attack the way in which I explain the targeting system as being "too technical" (whatever that means; see the Glossary). My experience is that truly interested persons are always willing to read to gain worthwhile information, and I am not about to underestimate a serious bowler's ability to understand printed material presented in an orderly, illustrated fashion. You, dear reader, serious and perceptive bowler that you are (or that you will become), are neither a beginner nor are you uninterested. So, please press onward to better bowling!

The parallel line targeting system fits nicely into the general scheme of this book. As you remember, I began by discussing how the grip, with its characteristic spans, pitches, hole sizes, and contours, dramatically affects the swing. The next logical step was to discuss the release in terms of leverage at the foul line. In that chapter, called "The Release", I chose not to become preoccupied with an involved discussion of the delivery, saving this unique and interesting subject for possible discussion in another book. With the present chapter, you have reached the point at which you should ask, "All of this information is very interesting, but what can I do with it?" Well, this chapter is going to help you get lined up on various target lines, the next two chapters will explain what happens to the ball as it is rolling along that target line, and the chapter after that will tell you how to adapt your target line and bowling ball to the various types of lane conditions that you will encounter. It is as simple as that! Nuts and bolts, ham and eggs, the guts of the game — call it what you will and do with it what you desire!

I must emphasize that, for purposes of clarity, all illustrations are made in reference to the so-called "ideal" lane condition (see the chapter titled "Increasing Your Adaptive Range" for a complete description). The dependability of any targeting system breaks down on less-than-ideal conditions, and how a ball will react on any target line is profoundly influenced by the type of lane condition upon which that target line is superimposed. Therefore, I hope that a standardization will not leave anything to the reader's imagination with respect to the type of lane condition to which I refer when I describe the action of a ball on a given target line. Standardization (i.e. in this case, the ideal lane condition) is necessary for the limitations of the system to be understood.

Elements of the Targeting System

Most likely, you noticed the dots and arrows on the approaches and lanes the very first time you tried to bowl and wondered what was their purpose. Subsequently, the first bit of instruction you were given (from a friend or family member) was probably a simple, "Stand with your foot on this dot and roll the ball over that arrow." This method is often incorrectly referred to as spot bowling, and to most persons — even to many high-average bowlers — this is the extent of the usefulness of the dot/arrow system. In fact, many so-called instructors are not really familiar enough with the system to be capable of telling others how to benefit from it. This unfamiliarity may be the honest result of the great number of bowlers using their own vague versions. This just adds to the confusion and frustration of new students of the game.

Finally, the time has come to take stock of what we need to know. The essential ingredients of a systematic approach to parallel line bowling using the dot/arrow devices are:

1. **The distance from the center of the sliding foot to the center of the ball in the swing.** I will call this the placement distance, and it is the distance in inches (or board widths) between planes 1 and 4 in Figure 19. Although this placement distance varies sufficiently in the population to be important in the choice a bowler makes in aligning with a particular target, it remains fairly constant for a lifetime.

2. **The size of the hook.** This factor will vary from lane to lane as well as from one type of condition to another (see chapter nine), and it must be accounted for before a target line is chosen.

3. **The relationship between the sets of dots and arrows on the approach and the lane and what number of boards these aids signify.** It is absolutely ludicrous to assume that you are targeting properly if you have no idea as to how these dots align with the arrows and upon which boards they lie.

4. **How to successfully integrate factors 1, 2, and 3, above, to develop a workable targeting system that is personalized for yourself and that will work in a majority of cases.**

5. **Any necessary modifications to the system.** These are made to accommodate problems such as a consistently crooked armswing and drifting (i.e. an approach line that deviates from the desired, either as a result of a consistent anatomical demand or as a result of the influence of different target lines). The chapter on adaptive range is devoted to the effects of different types of lane condition on the choice of target lines, and this will not be considered in any great detail in this chapter.

Let us now consider the ingredients more critically. The placement distance is very important because it establishes the important parallel relationship between the approach line (the tightrope that the bowler walks to the foul line) and the target line (the trajectory or vector that the ball will travel after it is released from the hand, i.e. the extension or continuance of the swing). Although this distance usually remains constant for a lifetime, it may change with great gain or loss of weight or with normal growth. It is generally larger for stocky persons and smaller for small persons with narrow shoulders, but it is also dependent upon the size of the hips, the structure of the legs, and the extent to which the bowling shoulder is dropped downward at the point of release.

To determine your own placement distance very simply, assume the finish position as shown in Figure 19, bend forward, and let the ball touch the floor. Measure the distance between the center of your sliding foot and the point at which the ball contacts the floor. It is expressed in boards or inches, one board = approximately 1 inch. Remember this distance for you will need to know it for as long as you bowl. If you are a growing youngster or are subject to wide fluctuations in weight, it may be necessary to make this determination from time to time to see if it has changed. If you consistently sidearm the swing, your placement distance is larger than that determined as I have described; someone will have to observe you to make the estimate of your placement distance. (It will become very apparent to you how important even the slightest inch deviation from the target can mean to the point where the ball contacts the pins.)

(*Author's Note:* Many individuals have a significant arm splay when observed from the front with arms to the sides and palms to the front. If such a bowler rolls the ball end-over-end, this characteristic can displace the touchdown (foul line) point of the ball to the outside, altering the desired target line; this error should be taken into account when selecting any target line.)

Determination of the size of the hook is probably the easiest to do for someone else but is not so easy to determine for yourself. I guess the reason for this is that, by the time the ball has begun to hook, the bowler is more concerned with the ultimate point of contact with the pins rather than the location of the where the hook began. Anyway, you must make this determination, and all that has to be done is to subtract the number of the outermost board (i.e. closest to the channel) over which the ball rolls from the number 17, the numerical reference of that board that divides the strike pocket in two. For example, you notice that the farthest point that the strike ball travels to the right for a right-handed bowler or to the left for a left-handed bowler is the ninth board from the channel — board #9. Simply subtract nine from 17, and the result is eight — the size of the hook. The ball begins to hook when it reaches board #9 and contacts the pins as it reaches board #17. The hook size will vary with the lane condition, and, no matter how large or small, it will begin at different distances from the foul line (the break point). Generally, the later the hook (the farther down the lane the break point occurs), the sharper the hook and the more effective the pin-spilling capability. Remember the size of your hook in terms of board width, but keep in mind that it will vary whereas the placement distance usually will not.

Before I begin to describe the dot/arrow system, I would like to tell you a little something about the history of its development, complements of ABC Hall of Fame member and All-Star champion, Buddy Bomar. During the second world war, the Brunswick Corporation installed a prototype Rangefinder system in military bowling facilities in several parts of the country. Why was such an aid needed? Because, before the dots and arrows were inlaid, bowlers had to aim directly at the pins or, if they wanted a target closer to the foul line, they were forced to count boards and use the differences in board color to remind them where their target was. The rationale was that it was easier to hit a target closer to the bowler, and thereby accuracy could be increased. Better bowlers were using closer-in lane targets, so a standardized aiming aid for everyone seemed appropriate. Lowell Jackson played a major role in developing the Rangefinder system (presumably because of his own limited vision), and Buddy Bomar was responsible for adding the small dots located approximately six feet from the foul line. There were intended to benefit bowlers wishing to aim at a point closer than the set of arrows that are approximately 15 feet from the foul line. Originally, the arrows were placed in a row, straight across the lane parallel with the foul line, but eventually, they were repositioned in the present-day "dovetail" pattern. In older pamphlets, there appeared more complete discussions of the Rangefinder system than appear today in even the most modern texts. Sadly, this has left much of the utility of this valuable aid sitting on the shelf, so to speak, and a reevaluation is long overdue.

(***Author's Note:*** In a recent conversation, Bill Lillard affirmed that, although blocked lane conditions have made it easier to repeat shots, the Rangefinder is still a useful targeting aid that bowlers should know how to use.)

Next, we are going to look at some diagrams of an approach and lane that show some essential relationships and proportions that are important for an understanding of what is discussed later. Please observe Figure 21 carefully. It illustrates which dots align with corresponding arrows and pins. Also, note that the small dots at the six-foot level from the foul line do not perfectly align with the larger dots and the arrows. Proper use of combinations of these markers makes targeting much simpler than it was before their development. Figure 22 shows the relationships among the labeled sections of the lane and approach. For purposes of illustration, assume the bowler under consideration rolls a straight ball and begins his approach at the set of dots at the end of the approach. Sections A and C are approximately the same length, so lateral (side-to-side) distances at the end set of approach dots are equal to those at the level of the arrows.

Figure 21: *A Cutdown Version of the Bowling Lane and Approach* – Note how the pins align with the dots and arrows of the Rangefinder system. The numbers indicate the board width distance away from the right and left channels. The "X" denotes the 17th (strike pocket) board.

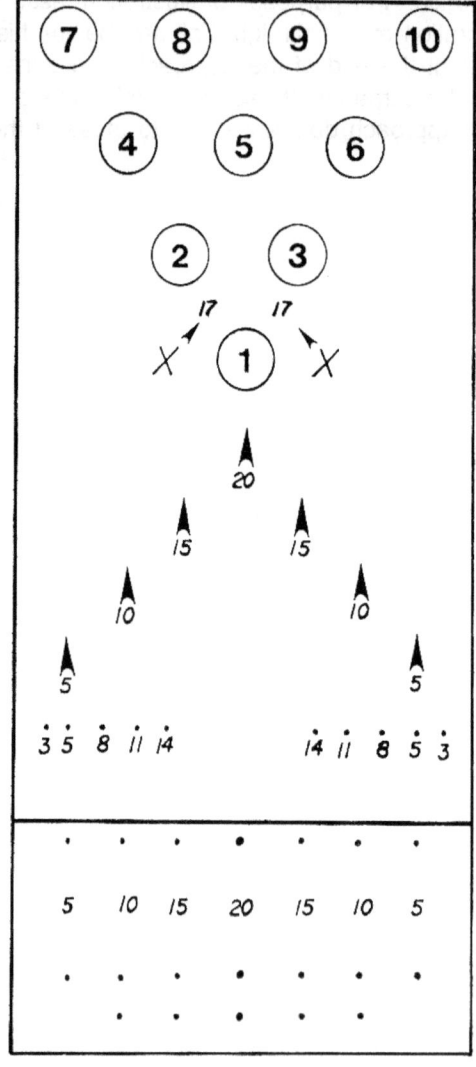

Figure 22: *A Roughly-scaled Diagram of the Lane and Approach* – Note the proportional relationships among the lengths of the sections.

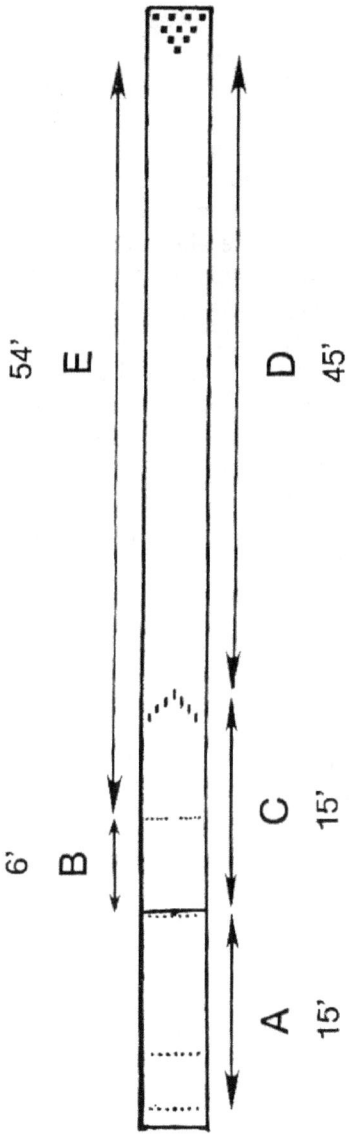

Since section D is three times as long as section C, a one-board error at the level of the arrows manifests a three board error at the level of the headpin. Beautifully logical, isn't it? Since section E is approximately nine times longer than section B, a one board error at the level of the six-foot dots manifests a nine-board error at the level of the headpin. Theoretically, the chance for error should be approximately three times as great when targeting at the six-foot dots as when targeting at the arrows (9-board error / 3-board error = 3), but in practice this is not the case. The reason is probably that greater accuracy is afforded by use of the near-in target and that proper alignment in the stance guarantees a certain amount of accuracy, regardless of where along his target line a bowler chooses to fix his eyes during the approach and delivery. Proponents of targeting at the arrows feel that a bowler reaches out or extends his followthrough more effectively when the target is further down the lane, but I, among many others, feel that the near-in target allows a more consistent release of the ball. The closer the target to the bowler, the easier it is to maintain the desired semi-squatted posture at the release. Since it is easier to see the near-in target than it is to see the arrows, arrow-level targeting promotes raising of the head and the trunk of the body at the release. I will deal with this subject again under "Use of the Target Point."

Playing Angles – The Elimination of a Popular Misconception

Suppose you are setting the ball down on board #10, and the ball rolls over the second arrow (i. e. it continues over the tenth board at the level of the arrows). Suppose further that the ball is hooking two boards too much. How much should you move your feet in the stance in order for the ball to hit the pocket squarely? If your answer was, "Two boards", you are guessing and are not ready to answer the question. I will forgive you this time, however, because "Two boards" is the answer that most persons will give. When you have finished this chapter, you will be able to figure out a more correct answer, and you will then have an obligation to those who answer "Two boards" to set them straight!

Let's define some terms. A playing angle consists of an approach line (the path of the steps), a target line (the vector or trajectory of the ball), and the stance position (the location of the center of the sliding foot at the beginning of the approach). Now, you know enough to understand how my philosophy of target line playing differs from most of the others. It is mainly built around the belief that the "spot bowler" such as it is defined in modern texts does not exist The original conception of a spot bowler was that of a person who attempted to set the ball down on a particular spot on the lane. The point of ball contact with the lane surface was considered to be the spot. Obviously, the spot could not be very far from the foul line, and naturally, spot bowlers utilized near-in targets. Over the years, authors vaguely defined a spot as "something a bowler aims at on a lane", "Rangefinder", "a target arrow on a lane", "mark on an alley at which bowler aims", etc. These definitions are optimistic, to say the least, they harken back to my original comment, "stand on this dot and throw at that arrow," and they are certainly inadequate!

The fact is that there is always some relationship between where a bowler stands on the approach and the point where he aims the ball, whether he is aware of it or not! Although it would be nice to be able to roll the ball at any target from any starting point on the approach, it is not really reasonable. Even though the bowler's ego may not allow him to accept it, he is limited as to what he can do from the very second he steps onto the approach. When he addresses the pins in the stance position, he is already on a target line of some type, because the target line extends all of the way to the back of the approach. He is lined up because the feet are pointed in some direction, a parallel relationship exists between approach and target lines, and logically, the target point (erroneously called the spot) lies somewhere on, or very close to the target line (see "Use of the Target Point").

Why try to do something that violates the established geometric relationship that already exists by choosing arbitrary target "spots" (there's that word, again) that you will miss most of the time due to improper alignment? Most likely, you will swear that you are rolling the ball over them and that you are a skilled "spot bowler" (whatever that is)! This kind of nonsense makes you no more accurate than a pin bowler (one who looks at the pins during his approach and delivery). What kind of an improvement is that?

I will make one last statement while stepping off of my soapbox for a little while. Some evening in the very near future, go to watch a league of better bowlers and notice how misdirected a great percentage of their deliveries are. When a bowler reaches a certain level of proficiency (a 180 average, for example), he really should not be misdirecting or "spraying" his shot very much. However, notice many different ways in which his ball contacts the pins. This is much more commonly the result of an improper choice of a target than is inconsistency in hitting the proper one. It is simply more difficult to consistently hit a target for which you are not properly aligned, and it seems that most bowlers choose the incorrect combination of beginning stance position and target line to fit their own, personal approach and swing. Picture it this way. Your approach line and target line represent railroad tracks. Your body's centerline plane and the plane of the swing (planes 1 and 4, Figure 20, A, respectively) represent the train's wheels. They must fit each other; the train must run on its appropriate set of tracks! Why should you not allow them to fit just so you can "stand on this dot and throw at that arrow?" *You are already a parallel line bowler, so why not use the system properly?*

Proper Use of the Rangefinder System

Let's play some different angles for hitting the pocket on the ideal lane condition. First, some more terms must be defined. The relative terms **inside** and **outside** refer to positions further away from and closer to the channel on the bowling arm side of the lane, respectively (see Figure 40). The **break point,** mentioned previously, is the point along the target line where the ball begins its hook; it is the place where the ball first deviates from the target line. It can be nearer to or farther from the bowler, depending on the lane condition. The **target point**, also mentioned previously, is the place on the target line at which the bowler fixes his gaze while approaching the foul line. The **foul line point** is that place along the target line where the ball contacts the lane, and the **arrow level point** is that place along the target line at the level of the Rangefinder arrows.

Some generalities stated here will apply to all of the playing angles. One is that, in the stance, the center of the sliding foot is perfectly aligned with the approach line (Figure 23 A, AL). Ideally, this is the case during the entire delivery. The bowling arm, however, will not align perfectly with the target line (Figure 23, TL) until the foul line release point is reached.

(*Author's Note:* During the last step, the swingside knee should bend deeply, ensuring a long slide. As a result, the sliding foot can come under the body's center of gravity, closing up the distance between the ball and the sliding foot, restoring the parallel relationship between the approach line and target line the correct distance (the placement distance) apart.)

The braking or balance leg will extend toward the back, leaving room for the ball to assume a position close to the ankle of the sliding foot. This will bring the ball back into alignment with the target line. These concepts are further clarified in the following discussions. Remember that any size of hook or any break point will accommodate just about any target line, but there are logical limitations that I hope are obvious after you have finished this chapter.

For purposes of the following six illustrations or cases, let's assume that your placement distance is six boards and that, because you choose to use different bowling balls or because you are more comfortable with a certain playing angle, the size of your hook is variable (i.e. you are capable of changing the size of the hook, depending upon what target line you desire to play).

Case 1: The 3-to-3 Target Line (Figure 23 A)

You determine that a comfortably-delivered ball hooks greatly (14 boards), and you prefer to use a straight-down-the-boards or straightaway angle because it favors your swing and bodily characteristics. This line is termed a 3-to-3 angle because you will set the ball down at the foul line three boards away from the channel, and the ball will roll over the third board at the level of the arrows. At some point down the lane (the break point), the ball will begin to hook, deviating from the target line, and you hope it will hit the pocket squarely as it rolls over the 17th board. If your ball leaves the target line early (the break point is relatively close to you), the angle of attack to the pocket will be shallower; if later (the break point is further away), the angle of attack will be steeper. If the angle is too shallow, deflection of the ball after contact with the pins is more apparent, but it is not as severe with such an extreme outside target line, If the angle is too steep, the ball will be too strong, and the tendency to leave corner pins (the 4, 6, 7, and 10 pins) is greater.

Since your placement distance is six boards, on what board will the center of the sliding foot be at the release? The ninth board, the same as in the stance, since this is a straightaway angle. The direction in which your feet are pointed in the stance is very critical. If you are fan-footed or pigeon-toed (sorry), you must determine how to place your feet to ensure that your approach line begins and ends at the two desired points. This is an individual matter, and it should not be neglected. Know precisely where you are on your approach line at all times!

Figure 23: *Three Outside Playing Angles*
A. A 3-to-3 target line
B. A 5-to-5 target line
C. An 8-to-8 target line

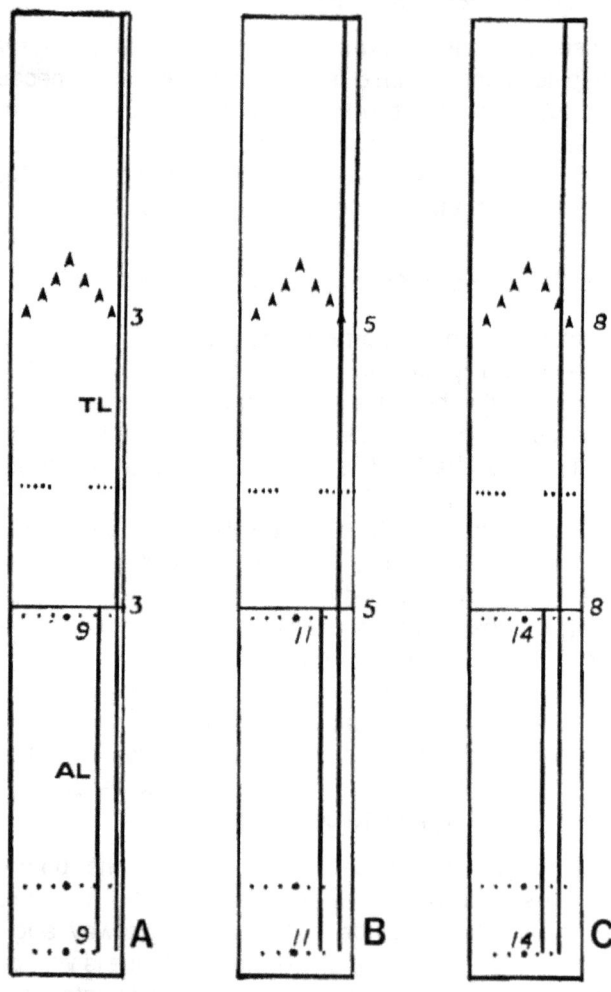

Case 2: The 5-to-5 Target Line (Figure 23 B)

This is an outside line. A comfortably-delivered ball hooks 12 boards, and you choose not to cut down the size of the hook. You desire to reach the fifth-board break point (17 − 12 = 5) with a straightaway angle, hence the 5-to-5 target line. This line is not as far outside as the 3-to-3 line, which could be used as effectively. In the case of a two-board smaller hook, the ball speed may be greater, the lift may be less, the ball weights and surface properties may favor less hook, and/or you may simply have chosen to adjust the hand position to make the hook smaller, necessitating the shift to the more inside target line.

In days gone by, this 5-to-5 line was about as far outside as anyone dared to play, but it is much more common today. This line requires that a person with a six-board placement distance keep the center of the sliding foot on the eleventh board of the approach.

Case 3: The 8-to-8 Target Line (Figure 23 C)

This is also an outside line. You choose to release the ball on the eighth board from the channel, and it crosses the level of the arrows while it is still on the eighth board. How many boards can the ball hook and still hit the pocket squarely? Nine boards (17 − 8 = 9). This line requires that the stance and release sliding foot position be the 14th board.

What would this position be if the placement distance were eight boards? It would be board #16, but the target line would remain the same! This is the reason that two bowlers can stand on different boards in the stance and still use the same target line (it is also a source of problems when one bowler tries to tell another how to play a certain lane)!

Although the 8-to-8 line is an outside type, it is usually close to, if not within, the limits of the track (see chapter nine). No track exists on the ideal lane, but realistically, it does exist on every lane, making the ball hook earlier (i.e. a closer break point). Furthermore, the closer to the 17th (pocket) board the target line becomes, the shallower the pocket attack angle becomes. Straightaway angles are more commonly used by bowlers who predominantly roll as opposed to turning the ball at the release. Since the shallower angles benefit from a later break point, a little more turn is effective in bringing this about. This subject is discussed in more detail when considering adaptive range.

Case 4: The 12-to-10 Target Line (Figure 24 A)

As you probably notice, this is the first example of a target line that is not straightaway. This type is generally termed in-to-out, the bowler being required to "belly the ball" out slightly. Now, I must make a very important point — *even though the target line is in-to-out, the swing always remains aligned with the target line and is still perfectly parallel with the approach line, no matter how diagonal the playing angle becomes.* Just because the ball is bellied out, this does not mean that the relationship between approach and target lines has changed. The only differences are that neither target nor approach lines are perpendicular to the foul line anymore; the target line now crosses the boards, and the bowler is no longer walking as directly toward the pins as he was with the straightaway lines. Although this 12-to-10 angle is not really very steep, it still requires a little thought to figure out the proper elements. For example, how large a hook could you predict with this line? Well, the answer is that it depends on the position of the break point. In the case of the straightaway lines (case 1, 2, and 3), It was a relatively easy matter to predict maximum hook size (for a pocket hit) simply by subtracting the number of the outermost board from the number of the pocket board. However, for the 12-to-10 line, what is the outermost board? If the break point occurs at the 30-foot level, it is board #8, two boards closer to the channel than at the arrow level. At the 45-foot level, the ball is on the sixth board (another two boards); and at the 60-foot level, the ball is on the fourth board (still another two boards, if the ball does not hook). Here is where knowledge of the location of the break point is important; how far down the lane does the ball hook? If the break point occurs at 45 feet, the hook size would be 11 boards (17 − 6 = 11); if at 30 feet, the hook size would be nine boards (17 − 8 = 9). Why would you not use a straightaway angle down the 11th or ninth boards? Personal preference; you may feel more comfortable with a slightly bellied target line, or the lane condition may require it for successful pin carry. Do you now see how important knowledge of both hook size and location of the break point can be?

Figure 24: *Three Inside Playing Angles*
A. A 12-to-10 target line
B. A 18-to-15 target line
C. A 22-to-18 target line

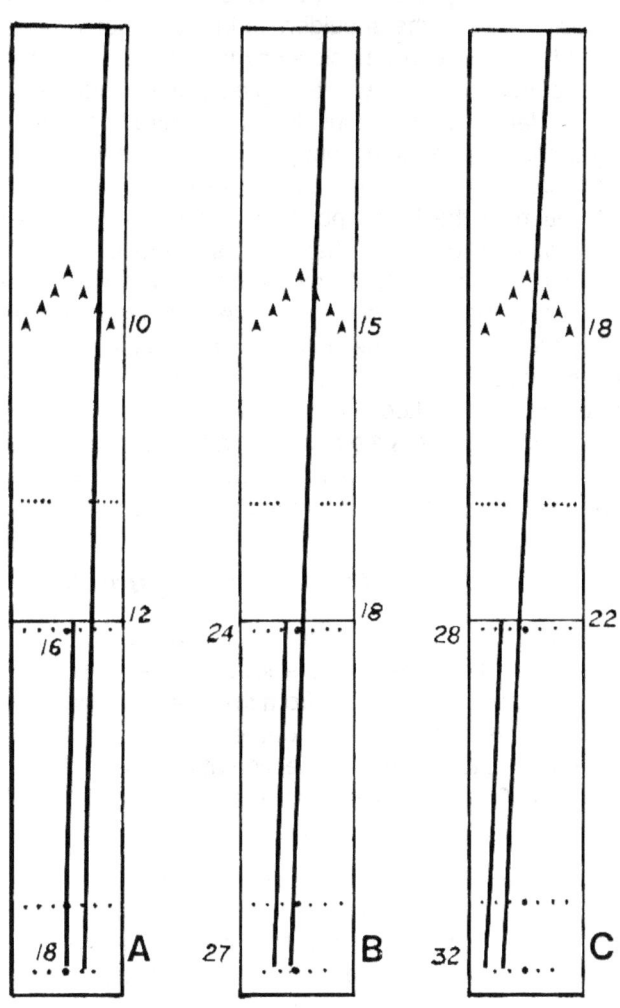

Case 5: The 18-to-15 Target Line (Figure 24 B)

This is a purely inside line, and, as you have already noticed, the target and approach lines remain parallel even though they are steeper and even more diagonal to the boards. The bowler using this (or any other angle that is not perpendicular to the foul line) must guard against turning the hips, thereby opening up his shoulders at the foul line. Opening the shoulders is the term used for pulling the shoulder of the bowling arm back, away from the target. Opening the shoulders effectively narrows the placement distance, and this displaces the target line to the inside of the desired position. This is a recurring problem for predominantly inside bowlers who seldom walk directly toward the pins. As in case 4, the size of the hook depends on the location of the break point, and the same calculations will apply, only with different numbers. This angle is slightly steeper, however, and consequently a ball traveling the 18-to-15 target line approaches the channel at a greater rate (a steeper angle) than the ball rolling on a 12-to-10 line (one board for each five feet of lane traveled as opposed to one board for every 7.5 feet; see "Determining the Size of the Hook or Location of the Break Point When One or the Other is Known". Where is the center of the sliding foot in the stance? It is on board #27 (with the six-inch placement distance) because the target line extends to board #21 at the back of the approach.

Case 6: The 22-to-18 Target Line (Figure 24 C)

This is an extreme inside line. The ball is placed on the 22nd board and crosses the 18th board at the level of the arrows. Since the arrows are approximately 15 feet from the foul line, what board would the target line intersect at the 30 foot level? The 14th board. How about the board of target line intersection at the row of dots at the end of the approach? It is the 26th board, and the stance position is on board #32.

The more inside lines are used more often by the big crankers (persons who lift and turn the ball strongly at the release, which results in a large hook). Also, with the 22-to-18 line, as was the case with the 18-to-15 line, it is easy to rotate the hips and open the shoulders, presumably because the bowler is walking an approach line that is even less directed toward the pins

The Out-to-In Target Line

This is a target line that is directed toward the pocket from a position further outside than the 17th board. It is justified only when used on lanes that do not allow a sufficient hook, such as extremely oily lanes. I do not recommend this type of line because it promotes a less-than-90-degree followthrough. Furthermore, it discourages the desirable rotary motion of the hand because the proper turn may result in a hit too high on the headpin.

Determining the Size of the Hook or Location of the Break When One or the Other Is Known

Please understand that I am not trying to impress you with these calculations. You may take these for what they are worth to you. They do serve to illustrate the differences between straightaway and in-to-out playing angles. Forgive me for getting a little technical, but some of you precocious readers may get a kick out of manipulating these figures!

To make these determinations, you must know what the playing angle is. In this illustration, let's use one that we have already discussed — the 12-to-10 target line. As you remember, these figures were given:

Lane Level	Board Number of Target Line Intersection
0 (Foul line)	12
15 feet	10
30 feet	8
45 feet	6
60 feet	4

To derive the rate at which the ball is approaching the channel, subtract one level from another and the respective board numbers from each other. This gives, for example:

$$45 - 30 / 6 - 8 = 15 / -2 = -7.5$$

which means that, for every 7.5 feet that the ball moves down the target line, it moves one board closer to the channel. The negative number indicates that the distance between the target line and channel is getting smaller; a positive number indicates that it is getting larger — the out-to-in line.

How can you determine the location of the break point from these data? If you know that the ball was set down on the 12th board and that the size of the hook has been observed to be ten boards, then the following assumptions can be made:

A. the outermost board is board #7 (17 − 10 = 7)

B. the ball moved five boards closer to the channel (12 − 7 = 5)

C. this equation is appropriate:

$$7.5 = B / 5, B = 37.5$$

The break point is 37' 6" from the foul line if the ball hooks ten boards from a 12-to-10 target line!

It is just as easy to figure the size of the hook when the location of the break point is known. Suppose that the break point is 45 feet from the foul line and N represents the number of boards that the ball has moved closer to the channel in that 45 feet:

$$7.5 = 45 / N, N = 6$$

This means that the ball has moved 6 boards closer to the channel than the point of origin, the 12th board. The outermost board is the sixth board (12 − 6 = 6), so the hook size must be 11 boards (17 − 6 = 11), because we subtract the number of the outermost board from the number of the pocket board. This is exactly the figure we obtained by drawing the line on the lane and observing what boards the target line intersected! You can test the logic behind the target line system.

Troubleshooting the Target Line System

The following is a summary of what we have learned so far with a few refinements added.

Choosing a Target Line: Always make it your business to know how large a hook a particular lane demands for a comfortably-delivered ball to hit the pocket. If you had a nice bird's eye view of the lane, you would draw a straight line from the break point to the pocket, and you could conceivably choose almost any target line to reach the break point, On the Ideal lane condition, you could choose the type of target line that is most comfortable for you — the type that you prefer to use most often from house to house — because it best fits your own stature, height, speed, etc. Deviating from the ideal situation for a moment, certain lane conditions may not favor certain target lines. If these are the playing angles that you do not like to use anyway, then all is fine. But, if the number of playing angles on the lane in question is restricted to those that you are not comfortable with, then you may have a problem! You must become adept at using all lines, developing more depth in your game.

The Problem with Modern Bowling Pins

I guess it is about time for me to climb back onto my soapbox. In recent years, innovations have made the pins more reactive when hit; they have been hollowed out, and the new plastic coats are more resilient. All of this has resulted in a wider leeway for the strike. The ball just simply does not have to hit the pocket as precisely as before to strike. Also, most lane conditions that have any scoring potential at all approximate the blocked condition; more oil is in the center of the lane than on the outside areas. This is grossly unfair to bowlers whose anatomy and swing characteristics favor the inside playing angles, because blocking obliterates those lines.

Another unfair aspect is that a present-day bowler can be scoring high after only a few months (of medium practice) at the game. This is because a turned ball delivered at medium speed on about a 12-to-10 target line is all that is necessary to hit the pocket on blocked lanes. The pins are less resistant, so good leverage, resulting from months of muscle development, is not necessary. The skillful bowler who can bowl from any target line, because he has spent long hours at his bowling apprenticeship, is pulled down to the level of the overnight superstar, the block specialist! For now, the block specialist is calling the rules of the game, because he has honed his delivery to match a very limited condition that really does not favor the adaptive bowler.

Well, I say to these overnight sensations, **"Enjoy your fun while you can!"** The ABC will impose more restrictions on pin design, and lane finishes will finally be developed that can make the sport more challenging. This turn of events will favor the serious, working bowler once again. Pin reactivity will come back down to earth, and blocking will not be necessary to provide a decent shot for everyone. I warn you of this because, if you are one of these superstars; your shot, your pride-and-joy, your ace-in-the-hole, will disappear! If you want to continue to score well, you must learn different target lines; you must learn to be a bowler — not a chunker. Heed my advice and learn this chapter, as well as the entire book, well!

(**Author's Note:** The American Bowling Congress reorganized into the United States Bowling Congress and continues to carry out business without having imposed any significant restrictions on bowling pins.)

Changing Target Lines to Accommodate Changing Lane Conditions: On the ideal lane, the condition never changes, no matter how many balls are delivered on it. However, both you and I know that lane conditions do change during the day and in proportion to the amount of play on them. Even while you are bowling in league, you find it necessary to shift your stance position and/or target line as the session progresses. I will not tell you when to change your angle. Rather, I will show you the relationships that you will need to know to change your angle sensibly.

With greater and greater amounts of play on a lane, the lane — especially the track — begins to slow down; the ball begins to hook more and sooner, the break point moves closer to the bowler, and the ball tends to hit too high on the headpin. In general, this usually necessitates a gradual shift of the target line to a more diagonal one, i.e. from 12-to-10 to 12-to-8 or 14-to-10, etc. Let's consider three cases. The first (Figure 25 A) shows the beginning target line, the one that you chose when the league play commenced. As play progresses, you feel the need to change to a more diagonal playing angle. You can change either or both of two points — the place where the ball first contacts the lane (the foul line point) and/or the place where the ball crosses at the level of the arrows (the arrow level point). Whether you decide to keep the arrow level point the same and roll the ball over the second arrow, or if you decide to keep the foul line point the same and change the arrow level point, **you must move your feet**. How much must you move your feet? If you decide to change the arrow level point, **for every board the arrow level point is moved, you must move your feet one board in the opposite direction**. This represents a 1:1 relationship, because the target line pivots on the foul line point that is equidistant from the arrows and the last set of dots at the end of the approach (I am assuming that your approach begins that far back.). If you decide to change your initial 12-to-10 line to a 12-to-8 line, how much would you have to move your feet in the stance? From the 20th to the 22nd board (assuming a 6" placement distance). Notice that the stance position shift is a positive one — a +2 board adjustment; the target line adjustment is -2 boards at the level of the arrows. This is shown in Figure 25 B.

86

Figure 25: Adjusting the Target Line Around a Foul Line (B) and Around an Arrow-level (C) Pivot Point

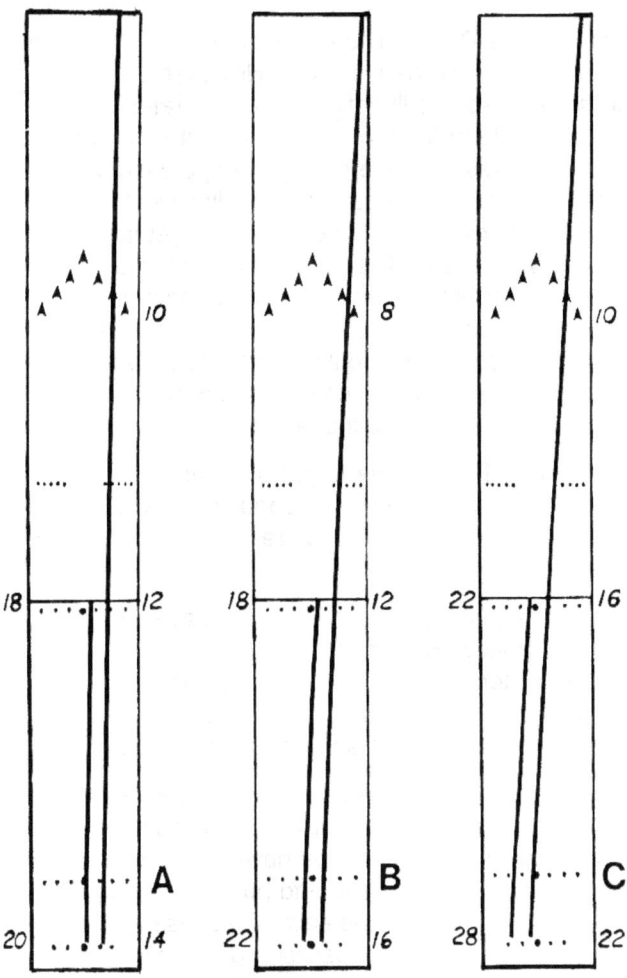

Suppose you decide to keep rolling the ball over the second arrow but you want to move your feet to compensate for the ball hitting the headpin too squarely. How many boards would you move your stance position to make a change in the target line from 12-to-10 to 16-to-10? You must move your feet eight boards — a 2:1 relationship — from the 20th board to board #28, a +8 adjustment. In this case, the target line has pivoted at the arrow level point that is 30 feet from the dots at the back of the approach. Figure 25 C shows the simple geometry involved. Do not try to make it more complicated than it actually is.

Use of the Target Point: The target point is what modern bowling books attempt to define as the spot. However, as you remember, I feel that the term spot is ill-defined, so I will refrain from using it. I prefer to use the term target point because it implies that the place where a bowler fixes his gaze during the approach and delivery lies somewhere on, or very close to, the target line itself. The spot can be assumed to be anywhere, whether on the target line or not! Where should you fix your gaze? The answer is not simple. Actually, if your body is aligned correctly with your playing angle, it should make no difference where you look — but it does! You may choose to look at the arrows, at the dots, at the foul line, or at any place in between any two of these. The important consideration is that the target point should be reasonably close to the target line.

(***Author's Note:*** Think of the target point as a "lure" to encourage you to walk to the same place at the foul line. Also, the target point stabilizes the head, neck, and posture. Then, you actually bowl by "feel.")

I use a system that has helped me increase my accuracy, and, according to Buddy Bomar, it is the proper way to use the Rangefinder system. The recommended method is to use the approach dots and lane arrows to align your body and then use the dots at the six-foot level (or closer) as your target point.

Notice, in Figure 21, that these dots do not perfectly align with the arrows. I feel that it is much easier to control the swing and to deliver the ball smoothly, keeping the hips down and the knees bent when using a near-in target point. I tend to pull my body up at the release when targeting at the level of the arrows because I have a rather crisp delivery with a relatively high backswing. Besides, if you need to make a slight correction to your target line to compensate for a temporary pull, this problem is both easier to diagnose and to correct with the near-in target point. Use of the six-foot level dots allows one to move the target point slightly inside or outside of the target line without moving the approach line. This can realign the ball trajectory with the target line without making any other adjustment in the playing angle. Sometimes you are tired, and the tendency is to pull the ball in toward the center of the body; the use of the near-in target point makes correction easier.

Figure 26: Modifying the Stance Position to Compensate for a Divergent Swing

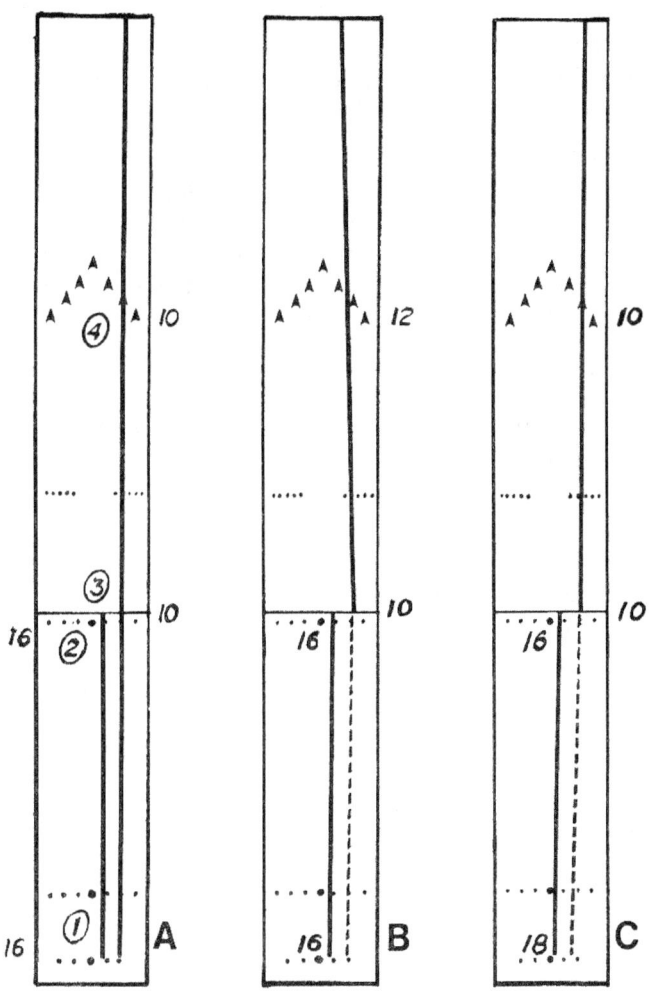

Modifying the Stance Position to Compensate for an Aberrant Swing: Very few persons exhibit a perfectly parallel relationship between approach and target lines. Therefore, some more adjustments have to be considered to fine-tune your playing angles.

89

Have a competent instructor observe your approach and the trajectory of the ball. Use a simple 10-to-10 target line, and have him make notes on paper, recording four points for each strike ball: the stance position of the sliding foot, the foul line sliding foot position, the foul line (target line) point and the arrow level (target line) point (see the circled numbers, Figure 26 A). Have him make these determinations for at least twenty deliveries to obtain an average for each point. This will allow both of you to observe a trend, and from this data, you can learn one of three revelations:

1. Your approach and target lines are perfectly parallel (Figure 25 A and Figure 26 A). If this is the case, good for you! The concepts of targeting that we have discussed apply more closely to you, and no additional adjustments are necessary to compensate for your swing. Notice that I did not say anything about drift; this is discussed in a later section.

2. Your target line converges with the approach line (Figure 26 B). If both lines were extended onto the lane surface, they would cross; the distance between target and approach lines becomes smaller — a negative error. A positive compensation (+, i.e. adding boards) in the stance position is necessary.

3. Your target line diverges from the approach line (Figure 27 B). If both lines were extended onto the lane surface, they would get farther apart with distance; this represents a positive error because the space between approach and target lines becomes larger. A negative compensation (i.e. subtracting boards) in the stance position is necessary.

How must you compensate? If you do not drift appreciably, then a simple adjustment can be made around a foul line pivot point. The point at which the ball is set onto the lane is consistently correct because the approach line is correct. Therefore, alignment of the ball trajectory is necessary to superimpose it on the desired target line: the approach line will have to be modified from the correct to the incorrect! Compensation for the swing can be made, therefore, by moving the feet in the stance position. This compensation, expressed in board number shift (adding or subtracting boards to the number of the board of the stance position), is a factor that is needed as long as your swing is not parallel with the approach line. If the parallel relationship is restored through diligent practice, the compensating factor will no longer be necessary.

Figure 27: Modifying the Stance Position to Compensate for a Convergent Swing

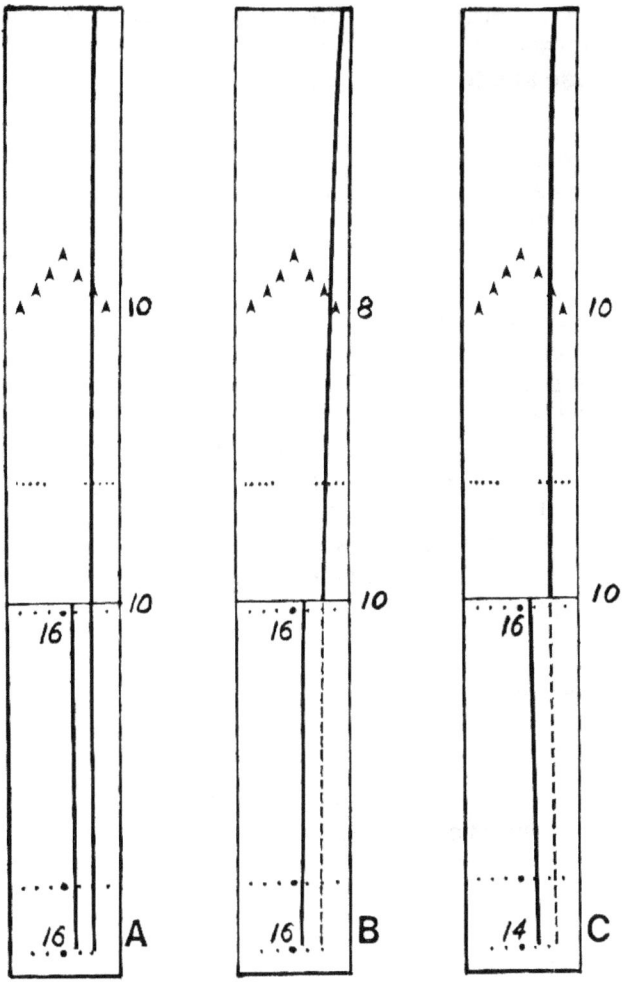

If your swing is convergent, the backswing probably flares out, away from the body (a common condition in bowlers with wide hips or who employ predominantly outside lines), and you may consistently miss your arrow level target to the inside. If you miss the arrow level point two boards inside, your target line is effectively changed from 10-to-10 to 10-to-12; if your placement distance is 6", what are the beginning and ending points of the approach line? Both are on board #16. Where must you assume your stance to adjust the target line back to 10-to-10? The center of the sliding foot should be shifted to board #18 — a +2 board correction to offset the -2 board error in the target line (see Figure 26 C). You would fix your gaze on the same target point, and the ball should travel the desired 10-to-10 target line. **You will use this two-board compensation anytime you play this target line.**

Suppose your swing is divergent. This probably is the result of the backswing being brought too far behind the back — a common condition in bowlers who use predominantly in-to-out lines. The arrow level point will be missed to the outside. If the point is missed two boards to the outside, shifting the 10-to-10 target line to 10-to-8, this represents a +2 board error that requires a -2 board compensation in the stance position. Two boards are subtracted from the stance board number. This is shown in Figure 27 C. In both cases, I have extended the target line onto the approach with a dotted line. This indicates that the swing is neither straight nor parallel with the approach line. I cannot say what the swing does during the approach, but it always results in a target line that is broken at the foul line. The take-home lesson is that a compensation is appropriate, necessary, and it can be figured easily if someone will help you gain the data you need. At the end of this chapter are forms that will help you.

Modification of the Stance Position to Compensate for Drift: Drift is defined as a deviation of the footwork from a desired approach line.

(**Authors Note:** It is important to determine that drift is not being misinterpreted. Bowlers who do not bend the swingside leg deeply enough, pushing into the slide will often step to the opposite side, making the sliding foot cross a board inside of the desired approach line. This is not drift and should not be compensated for as discussed below. Rather, an adjustment to footwork, allowing for a deeper knee bend of the swingside leg is in order. However, drift is often the result of a strongly aberrant swing, the ball swinging anti-parallel making the steps deviate from the desired approach line.)

The compensating factor is not as simple to determine as that for the swing because the type of playing angle employed influences the amount and direction of drift. Although drift may be related to the amount of swing deviation, it is more profoundly influenced by what angle you are playing. The amount of drift must be determined for each target line if you are going to further fine-tune your target system.

As opposed to the swing that is relatively consistent in relation to the approach line, the drift is inconsistent, sometimes one direction, sometimes another, depending upon whether an inside or outside playing angle is used. You must resign yourself to the fact that such inconsistencies exist in the game of an adaptive (experienced and skillful) bowler, but, if these inconsistencies are properly compensated for, inconsistency can be minimized, and accuracy can be increased.

Although some bowlers are blessed with a drift-free approach, I have, to my knowledge, never met one; and certain generalities can be made. When playing extreme diagonal (inside) lines, there is a tendency for the approach line to converge with the target line (i.e. a right-handed bowler drifts to the right). This is a negative (-) error that requires a positive (+) correction. When playing extreme outside straightaway lines, the approach line tends to diverge from the target line (i.e. a right-handed bowler drifts to the left). This is a positive (+) error that requires a negative (-) correction. These tendencies are even more severe the greater the deviation of the playing angle from the one to which the bowler is accustomed. Such drift changes the playing angle by shifting the target line release point; the placement distance remains the same. The ball is delivered to the left or right of the desired foul line point, and the ball may or may not roll over the arrow level point. By using data gained in the same manner as that for the swing compensation factor, you can develop drift compensation factors. Truly, the instructor's observations may take a while to make, but once he has completed them, he should not have to do them again, unless you want to see if any factors have changed. It would be nice if you could commit them to memory, but if you can't, copy them down and take them with you when you bowl. In the heat of bowling competition, it is tempting not to concern yourself with details, but if you start out using the correct positions, you will be way ahead in terms of playing the lanes properly.

For clarity, I will use the same playing angles that we have previously discussed. Assume that the placement distance is six boards (inches) and that the ball hooks into the pocket, hitting squarely with each line. At the end of this chapter are forms that will help you develop your own swing and drift compensation factors

I think that the points are best illustrated by comparing the drift patterns of two bowlers. Consider Table 1. It has been filled in with data (the average of several trials) gained in a hypothetical, instructor-observed practice session.

Table 1: Compensation Factors for Two Bowlers Using the Same Six Playing Angles

Target Line	(A)	(B) Ideal Stance	(C) Ideal F.L.	(D) Actual Stance	(E) Actual F.L.	(F) Amount Of Drift (E-C)	(G) Drift C.F. (-F)	(H) Swing C.F.	(I) Combined Stance (B+G+H)
Bowler	3-to-3	9	9	9	11	+2	−2	−2	5
#1	5-to-5	11	11	11	13	+2	−2	−2	7
	8-to-8	14	14	14	15	+1	−1	−2	11
PD = 6"	12-to-10	20	18	20	17	−1	+1	−2	19
	18-to-15	27	24	27	22	−2	+2	−2	27
	22-to-18	32	28	32	25	−3	+3	−2	33
Bowler	3-to-3	9	9	9	7	−2	+2	−2	9
#2	5-to-5	11	11	11	9	−2	+2	−2	11
	8-to-8	14	14	14	13	−1	+1	−2	13
PD = 6"	12-to-10	20	18	20	18	0	0	−2	18
	18-to-15	27	24	27	25	+1	−1	−2	24
	22-to-18	32	28	32	30	+2	−2	−2	28

Compensation Factors For Two Bowlers Using The Same Six Playing Angles: Columns A through I are explained below. PD = placement distance, F.L. = foul line position, C.F. = compensation factor.

- A. Target Lines as explained previously (see figures 23 and 24)
- B. The sliding foot stance position appropriate for the target line and a PD of 6"
- C. The foul line sliding foot position appropriate for the target line and a PD of 6"
- D. The actual stance position used by the bowler should always be the appropriate one.
- E. The actual foul line sliding foot position usually deviates from the ideal one.
- F. The amount of drift is the actual minus the ideal foul line sliding foot positions.
- G. The drift compensation factor is the algebraic opposite of the amount of drift.
- H. For purposes of this table, assume that both bowlers exhibit similar divergent swing of two boards which require a −2 board correction (see figure 27)
- I. The adjusted sliding foot stance position appropriate for the target line in question for this bowler. This takes into account both swing and drift characteristics, i.e. the ideal stance position with both factors added algebraically.

Notice that both bowlers are playing the same target lines and are assuming the same stance positions (ideal). However, their approach lines end at the foul line at different points for individual target lines. In short, their drift patterns are different. (These differences, as you will notice, violate the generalities that I discussed previously. I must be honest, because generalities do not apply to everyone.). I could diagram these as I have before, but this would mean that you must look at eight more illustrations, and I think you know enough now to envision playing angles by looking at the numbers on the chart. Both of these bowlers are off their approach tracks! Should they quit in disgust? No, just as you should do, they will calculate for success! By subtracting the actual foul line sliding foot positions from the ideal ones, we derived the numbers in column F. Negative numbers indicate drift toward the target line, and as with the convergent swing, this represents a negative error (the space between the two lines becomes smaller) that requires a positive correction. Positive numbers indicate drift away from the target line, a positive error, and a negative compensation factor. Column G is simply the degree of drift with the signs changed — the drift compensation factor. It is read as that number of boards added or subtracted to the number of the board upon which is placed the sliding foot in the stance; they correspond to the target lines indicated in column A. The drift compensation and swing compensation factors can be added to each other to give a combined factor for each target line! For example

(-2) + (-1) = -3 and (+3) + (-2) = +1, and so forth.

The swing compensation factor (column H) will be assumed to be -2 for both bowlers, and the adjusted stance position can be seen in column 1.

Before you apply any compensation factors for drift, you would do well to try to determine the cause. If the problem is a simple one, then an attempt to correct this problem would be in order before compensations are made.

(*Authors note:* A simple solution might be to move the ball in the stance to a position in front of the swingside shoulder, for example.).

If you can eliminate the cause, it is always better to do so than to cope with it. If the solution would involve too much time, then a compensation is appropriate.

Some Questions to Test Your Understanding of the Targeting System

1. If you are using a 15-to-10 target line with a straight ball, how far from the foul line will the ball fall into the channel?
2. You have an 8" placement distance. Your stance board is #28, and your slide ends on the 21st board. What ideal target line are you playing?
3. With a 22-to-18 target line and a break point 52 feet from the foul line, what is the size of a pocket-hitting hook?
4. What is the theoretical maximum size of the hook of a perfect strike ball on a 22-to-20 target line?
5. Assume that your placement distance is 7 boards. Your instructor tells you to stand on the 20th board and to roll the ball on a 13-to-10 target line.
   a. What is he asking you to do?
   b. What is going to happen?
   c. Is the instructor's request valid?

Answers

1. 45 feet. The ball rolls over the 15th board at the foul line, over the 10th board at the level of the arrows, over the fifth board at the 30' level, and finally into the channel just as it passes the 45' level.

2. 13-to-6. If we extend the target line onto the approach and subtract the placement distance from the approach points, we get 20 and 13. Therefore, 13 is the foul line point on the target line. Since the approach points indicate a 7-board diagonal, and since approach and target lines are parallel, the arrow level point of the target line must be board #6.

3. Nine boards. Using the equations previously discussed, we found that the ball moves one board closer to the channel for every 3.7 feet of distance traveled. If the break point is 52 feet from the foul line, then the ball moves 14 inches closer to the channel from the original point of origin, the 22nd board. 22 – 14 = 8, the outermost board! Therefore, if we subtract the number of the outermost board from the pocket board number, we see that the size of the hook is nine boards (17 – 8 = 9).

4. Three boards. However, this is theoretical and very impractical! Since the ball hits the target line at board #22 and travels, within 15 feet, to the 20th board, it must roll over the 18th board at the 30' level, over the 16th board at the 45' level, and the 14th board at the 60' level. 17 − 14 = 3 boards of hook, but the ball would cross the 17th board at such a steep angle that a strike would be out of the question!

5. a. He is asking you to put your sliding foot on the center board of the approach at the stance and to roll your ball in the direction of the second arrow, with the ball making initial contact with the lane on board #13.

 b. Something undesirable is most likely going to happen! If your placement distance is seven boards and if you endeavor to maintain a parallel relationship between approach and target lines, your sliding foot must be on the 20th board at the foul line for you to put the ball down on board #13. You can roll the ball over the tenth board at the arrows, but this requires that you either change to a different stance position so you can retain the 13th board foul line point or you must be content with a 10-to-10 target line. There may be one exception to this situation; see c., below.

 c. Generally speaking, this request is not valid, because it does not allow for maintaining a parallel relationship between approach and target lines. The only exception would be if the instructor were making a compensation for your swing and/or your drift. In this case, he would have to be assuming that you drift three boards away from your target line. If this were so and if your swing naturally bellied the ball out toward the channel at the rate of three boards per 15 feet of travel, then his request would be valid. If you do not heed my words, *"Know thyself," you may waste a lot of time attempting to play angles suggested by others. Ask yourself first, "Is that a valid request; is that angle appropriate for me?" Instructors beware!*

What's all of the Fuss About Shooting Spares?

This section involves what I am not going to say about shooting spares rather than what I could say! So much has been written about this subject that I feel that numerous diagrams that illustrate many different spare conversions would not add much to your present knowledge. I can contribute to, simplify, and enhance your spare-shooting capabilities just by pointing out a few things that can be easily related to that which (I hope) you have already learned from this chapter. These are listed below.

1. The only important fact to remember in shooting spares is that you want the ball to hit an individual pin squarely or to roll directly between two adjacent pins. The 4-5 split is actually a 2-pin spare, the 3-10 split is actually a 6-pin spare, the 3-5-6 is actually a 1-3 or a 3-6 spare, and so on. Keeping this in mind, all spare combinations are simplified into one-and two-pin spares based on the front pins, and only minor modifications of the stance position are necessary to accommodate variations of these spares. Refer back to Figure 21 and relate it to the information on Table 2:

Table 2: Board Numbers of Desired Spare Destinations at the Pins

Point of Impact Ball Path at Pin Level	# of Board	
	Left-Handed	Right-Handed
At the 7-pin	5	35
Between 4- and 7-pins	7-8	32-33
At the 4-pin	10	30
Between the 2- and 4-pins	12-13	27-28
At the 2-pin	15	25
Between the 1- and 2-pins	17-18	22-23
At the 1-pin	20	20
Between the 1- and 3-pins	22-23	17-18
At the 3-pin	25	15
Between the 3- and 6-pins	27-28	12-13
At the 6-pin	30	10
Between the 6- and 10-pins	32-33	7-8
At the 10-pin	35	5

As you can see, there are only thirteen ultimate points of ball contact with the pins!

2. In adjusting the stance position for spares, you may choose to pivot your target line on a particular point such as one at the level of the arrows. You can choose to use only a few pivot points such as the second arrow for one group of spares and the third for another group, etc. I have four or five pivot points with a couple of different stance positions for each, but I will not state here what they are because they may not be appropriate for you. It really does not matter what arrow level points you use for spares; the important thing is to find the best ones and use them consistently for the appropriate spares.

3. If you know the size of your hook on the lane, you can substitute the number of the board of desired ball contact for the number 17 in your strike ball angle, as we have discussed before.

4. You may still choose a target point anywhere along your spare-shooting target line; you may elect to use a near-in target point, an arrow level point, or anywhere else, as long as it is very close to the line.

5. Ask yourself questions like, "If I am right-handed and am shooting the 7-pin spare with a seven-board hook and a six-board placement distance, where must I stand to hit the pin by rolling the ball over the second arrow?"

(I'll answer this one; you will have to ask and answer your own when the time comes!). For a right-handed bowler, the 7-pin is set on the 35th board; if the hook size is seven boards, the break point occurs on board #28 (35 − 7 = 28). Although it would be nice to know the distance of the break point from the foul line, let's assume it is 45 feet, hence 30 feet from the arrows. This means that the arrow level point is equidistant from the break point and the last row of dots at the back of the approach. Therefore, a shift of one board in the stance will bring about an opposite one-board shift of the target line at the level of the break point (not at the arrows)! The target line extends from board #28 (the break point), pivots on board #10 (the second arrow), and ends on board # -8 at the back of the approach (10 − 18 = -8). Minus eight? Yes, this only means that your armswing begins eight boards to the right of the edge of the lane; your sliding foot is centered two boards to the right of the edge of the lane (i. e. -2)! Won't the ball wind up in the channel? No, not if you do not drift. The ball will be set down on board #1 (halfway between board #10 and board # -8); the sliding foot will stop on board #7. This illustration should reinforce your opinion against the "stand here and throw there" concept. What if you stood two boards further to the right? You would roll a gutter ball (oops, sorry — a channel ball)! What if you stood two boards to the left? You would either miss the seven pin, miss the break point, or miss the second arrow; you cannot hit all three!

Swing Compensation Data Form

In the form below, record the board numbers for 20 deliveries along a 10-to10 target line. Remember to take your placement distance into consideration.

PD = _____. Point 1 is the sliding foot stance board # position, and it should be identical for all 20 deliveries. Point 2 is the sliding foot board # position at the foul line. Point 3 is the foul line point of ball contact board #. Point 4 is the arrow level point board #. You should use an observer for points 3 and 4. See Figure 26 A.

Points #	Delivery #																				AVE
	1	2	3	4	5	6	7	8	9	10	11	12	13	14	15	16	17	18	19	20	
1																						
2																						
3																						
4																						

Judging from the average data above, my own swing _____ (converges toward/diverges away from) the target line at the level of the arrows. The ideal (with my placement distance of _____) positions for the 10-to-10 target line are as follows: point 1 _____, point 2 _____, point 3 _____, point 4 _____. The extent of error of my swing is _____ (+ or -) boards, and this requires a compensation factor of _____ (+ or -) boards repositioning of my stance.

My Own Personal Swing Compensation Factor is _____

Drift Compensation Data Form

Record only points 1 and 2 (see Swing Compensation Data Form) for ten deliveries per target line and compute the averages. See Table 1 for the ideal board numbers based on a 6" PD, and figure your own accordingly.

Target Line	Point	Delivery #										Ave
		1	2	3	4	5	6	7	8	9	10	
3-to-3	1											
	2											
5-to-5	1											
	2											
8-to-8	1											
	2											
12-to-10	1											
	2											
18-to-15	1											
	2											
22-to-18	1											
	2											

From the average data above, I can see that my drift pattern for the six target lines tested is as indicated below. Also included are drift compensation factors

My Own Personal Drift Compensation Factors

Target Line	Stance Position	Ideal F.L.	Actual F.L.	Amt of Drift	Drift C.F.
3-to3					
5-to-5					
8-to-8					
12-to-10					
18-to-15					
22-to-18					

Combining Swing And Drift Compensation Factors

My Own Personal Adjusted Sliding Foot Stance Positions For Six Different Target Lines

Target Line	Swing C.F.	Drift C.F.	Adjusted Stance Position
3-to3			
5-to-5			
8-to-8			
12-to-10			
18-to-15			
22-to-18			

Notes:

7 Weight Distribution within a Bowling Ball

(***Author's Note:*** The term, weight distribution refers to the amount and position of the weight center or center of gravity of a drilled bowling ball. Further definitions and explanations are found under the section heading, "Use of Imbalance." Modern bowling balls are marketed with different types of construction. Some are what I refer to as "shell-dense" are now called "high RG", RG standing for "radius of gyration." Others are what I refer to as "core-dense" are now referred to as "low RG." No matter what current marketing language is attached to these products, the principles are the same as when ***Perceptive Bowling*** was written; the dynamics described herein still apply.)

Personalities

When I think about weight distribution in bowling balls, four names come to mind. The first and foremost is J.D. Amburgey, a West Texan who, as early as the late 1950s, poured thousands of dollars into research on the effects of different placements of the weight center to achieve different roll characteristics of the ball on the lane. He hired physicists from nearby universities to conduct controlled experiments. He also sponsored teams of the best bowlers in the area, and these men used all different brands of balls and combinations of weights while the scientists analyzed the results. Further, they cut bowling balls into small pieces and studied the composition and density. In fact, armed with the information gained through these studies, Amburgey was even able to predict to within a few millimeters where the weight center would finally rest and the amount of weight imbalance at this location before the grip was drilled! He could, on certain lane conditions, predict what pins would be left on pocket hits. Further, if the weight center placement was correct, the ball would even seem to make a louder sound on impact than one with incorrectly-placed weight. All of his work was done at a time before plastic balls became popular and before even the best bowlers knew much about weight distribution. Modifications of his ideas have appeared at some time or another in every major brand of ball. For years, he has wanted manufacturers to make a bowling ball the way he feels is necessary for maximum hitting power. This design involves not only the amount of weight, but the shape of the weight block and the degree of compactness of the core, etc. Therefore, he manufactures a ball himself in a plant in Odessa, Texas, and the design promises the bowler who has the price of the ball a new perspective on the game.

Another prominent figure is Vincent "Viny" Yetitto, a fine veteran bowler from New York state. He invented the "Roto-Grip", which allowed one to alter the spans of a bowling ball as it was being used. (This invention went by the wayside when the American Bowling Congress (ABC) outlawed any movable parts in bowling balls.) More significantly, he, along with his son, Vincent Jr., has developed the Roto-Star balls. The main feature of these balls is that the label is placed off-center of the weight center at the factory so that positive side weight and finger weight (along with top weight) will result if the grip is drilled in the center of the label. These weights are indicated on the shipping carton, and the manufacturer can make these predictions based on the sizes of a person's fingers relative to the thumb and based on accurate knowledge of the imbalance resulting from shifting known top weight in predetermined directions before engraving the ball label. I am not convinced that everyone needs finger weight for all conditions, but as far as quality control Is concerned, the Roto-Star is unsurpassed. Vincent Sr. is now retired and living in Florida, but you can bet he is still in his workshop trying to resolve the many unanswered questions about bowling balls. Vincent Jr. is now the active head of the company. He has published and given lectures on the action of weight imbalance (he calls it the Weight Concept Theory). These publications, I understand, are available in Belgium and Japan but are unavailable in this country. I sincerely hope he will publish his works in this country; maybe this writing will prompt him to do so.

A third figure — one who has published extensively in the United States — is Bill Taylor, the "Coach to the Pros." I first became interested in him when I learned of his coaching function for members (especially for Steve Nagy) of the great disaster, the National Bowling League, in 1961. A confident man, he is now affiliated with BT Bowling Products in San Gabriel, California. Through this organization, he distributes his books, an axis-weighted ball named the "Side Roller," as well as many innovative devices designed to aid the driller or pro shop operator. I must refer you to his books for a detailed treatment of many different concepts. These publications are both entertaining and informative even though they do heavily promote his own products.

The fourth figure, the late W. J. "Red" Childers, was a personal friend. Although he never did any quantitative studies on weight distribution and surface properties of the ball, he knew as much about these subjects as any man I have ever known. It is reported that he purchased for himself over 400 new bowling balls during a two-year period, and it was not uncommon to see him bring five new balls at one time into the old Superior Bowling Club (on the Central Expressway in Dallas, Texas) to try them out. This experimentation cost him thousands of dollars, but he gained a tremendous amount of information. Through hours of conversation with him I learned a good portion of the lessons that have become the basis of this book. Because of the folklore surrounding Red, he was passed off as an eccentric by many. However, he was well-read, bright, honest, overly generous, and had a keen sense of humor. He will never be forgotten by those fortunate enough to have been his friends.

Bowling Ball Construction

Bowling balls are generally constructed in three parts. (The steps are presented, if oversimplified, in Figure 28.) The first part is the core that is a composite of various materials such as a barium metal salt, cork, masonite, fabric, etc. It is approximately six inches in diameter. The next addition is usually that of a weight block (a misnomer, since it is almost never cubical). This material is usually a barium salt that is denser (consequently, heavier) than the core material. It normally is a four or five-inch disc or "puddle" that is placed on the surface of the core.

Figure 28: Steps in The Manufacture of a Bowling Ball – The core (C) is made first, the weight block (W) is added, then the shell (S) is molded around them. The punch mark (PM) indicates the position of the weight center, and the label is engraved around the punch mark.

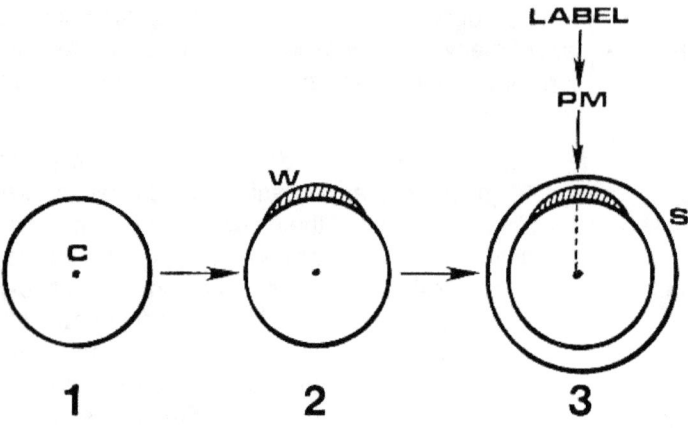

Lastly, the cover of rubber or plastic is molded around the core and weight block. The ball is weighed, the center of weight is stamped (the punch mark), and the label is engraved centered around the punch mark.

Use of Imbalance or Weight Center Shift

Before they are drilled, bowling balls are usually heavier in the top half than in the bottom half. This is called "having top weight," and this top weight results from the placement of the weight block in the manner described above. It is the drilling of the grip off of the weight center that creates the imbalance known as top/bottom, finger/thumb, and positive (the side of the hook) / negative (the side opposite the hook) lateral weights. When one drills off of the weight block center to create some sort of imbalance, it is termed weight center shift or, simply, weight shift.

Figure 29: Influence of Placement of the Weight Center on the Roll of a Semirolling Ball

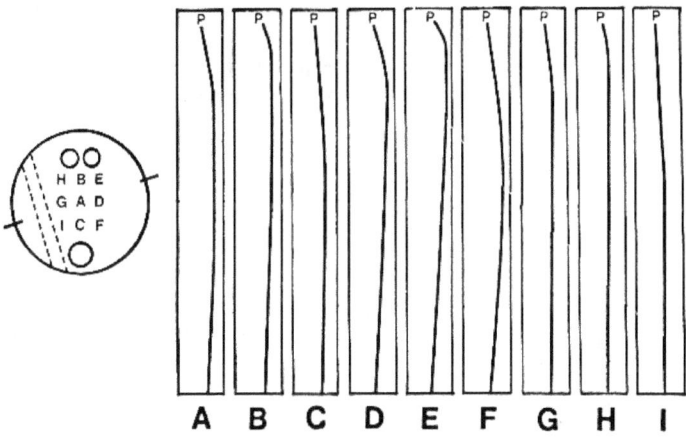

The influence of various weight center placements is illustrated by Figure 29 This is in keeping with concepts generally accepted today. However, I do not necessarily feel that these concepts are correct, and I recommend that you read Bill Taylor's ***Balance*** before forming any opinion. The letters represent the weight center relative to the grip as well as the effect of the hooking action on the ball. A, B, and C are conditions in which there is neither positive nor negative side weight. I have chosen these to depict moderate hooking action. D, E, and F represent positive side weight and maximum hooking action. G, H, and I represent negative side weight and minimum hooking action. The relative position and amount of finger/thumb weight to the grip as well as the track determines the location of the break point on the lane. Finger weight brings about a later hook than thumb weight if the track is not parallel with the grip layout centerline.

(***Author's Note:*** Actually, if the track is closer to the thumb than to the fingers, thumb weight brings about an earlier hook. If the track is closer to the fingers, thumb weight brings about a later hook.)

All of these examples are for the semirolling ball with a slanted track (dotted line) as shown in Figure 29. These generalities do not apply to the full roller, and this topic is discussed later The small "P" stands for "Pocket" (clever?). For the examples of Figure 29, it should be understood that each of the modifications to weight center position have been tested on the same lane. In other words, A through I are exactly the same lane condition. Further, when making conclusions concerning imbalance, the surface (and, preferably, the core) characteristics of the balls being tested should be the same (all rubber or plastic and of the same hardness and texture). Weight distributed within ABC tolerances begins to lose its effectiveness on extremely oily or dry lanes or within balls that are extremely hard or soft.

In addition to finger/thumb and lateral weight, there is still a quantitative top/bottom weight consideration (for our purposes, assume that the weight center is always two ounces in each example of Figure 29). The amount of shift necessary to obtain a desired finger/thumb or lateral weight is profoundly influenced by the amount of top weight available to shift. **Less shift of the weight center is necessary when there is more top (or bottom) weight in the undrilled ball.**

Incidental Weight Shift

The term incidental is used here to mean a weight center shift that is not necessarily planned by the driller. These shifts may be small, and they have been spoken of as insignificant in the literature. However, I feel that a word about them is necessary since no one has taken the time to explain them. When the grip is drilled around the punch mark, the actual weight center will move from a position under the mark in the direction toward the area where the lesser weight is removed. Figure 30 illustrates this shift. The statement holds true especially for fingertip grips where the fingerholes are drilled 1 1/2 inches deep and the thumb hole is drilled 2 1/2 inches deep (standard depths).

Figure 30: Movement of the Weight Center After Drilling a Fingertip Grip Around the Punch Mark (PM) — This is the incidental "hole size weight shift." The weight center moves in the direction where less material is removed.

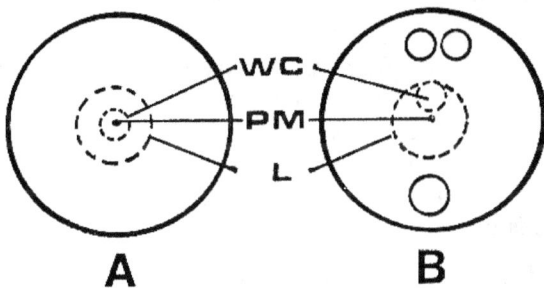

Consider the hypothetical grips in Figure 31.

Figure 31: A Comparison of the Fingertip Grip (A) With the Conventional Grip (B) with Respect to the Amount of Weight Removed by Drilling the Holes—The fractions denote the hole diameter in inches.

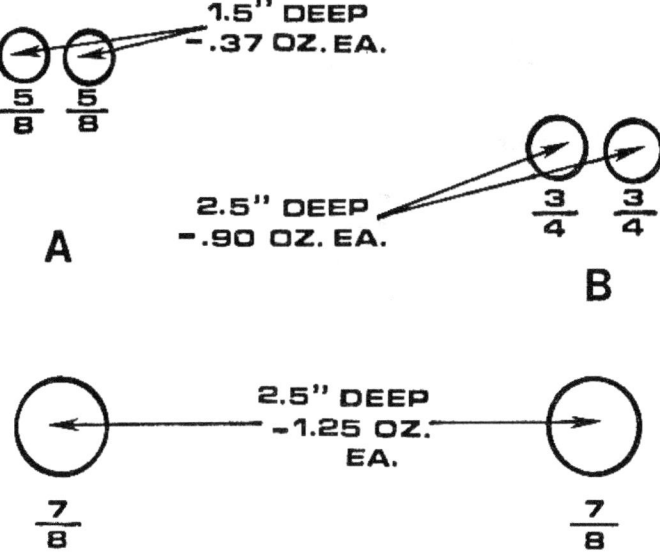

Actually, the ring finger is usually smaller than the middle finger, but for ease of illustration I made them the same size. In A (fingertip grip), the total weight removed by the fingers is 0.74 ounces. This is less than the 1.25 ounces removed by drilling the thumbhole, so 0.51 ounces of finger weight would result (1.25 – 0.74). In B (conventional grip), the total weight removed by the fingers is 1.80 ounces. This is greater than the 1.25 ounces taken from the thumbhole, so 0.55 ounces of thumb weight would result (1.80 – 1.25). This shift I call hole size weight shift, and it must be considered before attempting to shift the weight center. There are intermediate conditions of hole size weight shift, and there may even be occasions when the weight center will not shift at all. Remember that centering the grip over the punch mark does not mean that the grip is centered over the weight center of the ball. If the grip is drilled with the center on the punch mark, some finger or thumb weight usually results.

Another shift of the weight center occurs in response to the pitches and depth of the holes. The weight center will tend to shift in the direction of pitch. The degree of this shift is greater with increasing pitch and hole depth. A table showing this effect is included in the back of the chapter on drilling. Most persons use forward fingerhole and reverse thumbhole pitch. This effect tends to cancel the effects of hole size weight shift. This is probably the reason why both effects have been considered insignificant and their amounts negligible. These shifts do exist, however, and they are included so you can decide for yourself their importance.

Bottom Weight

I have purposely biased my discussion of top/bottom weight in favor of top weight. It is only in rare circumstances that anyone uses bottom weight. I am not certain of the effects of bottom weight on the skid, roll, and hook; but I believe that most professional bowlers prefer that the weight center, apparently for less deflection at impact, be between the hand and the geometric center of the ball. Figure 32 shows how to shift the center of bottom weight to achieve

Figure 32: Positioning of the Center of Bottom Weight (BW) Relative to a Right-Handed Grip to Achieve Lateral Weight (A) and Finger/Thumb Weight (B)

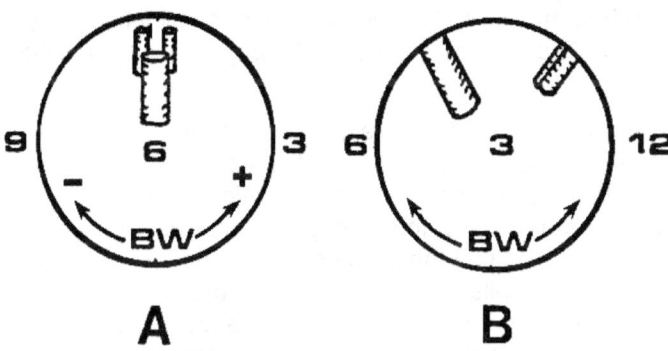

positive/negative lateral and finger/thumb weight for a right-handed grip. Naturally, one would start with a ball that has very low top weight before drilling. In all cases, one will still have a bottom-weighted ball. Bottom weight shift can still be figured according to charts and devices designed for use with top weight, but what must be remembered is that drilling the holes actually adds to bottom weight while diminishing top weight.

Top Weight

The amount of top weight to use is highly conjectural. Most drillers view top weight as simply that amount available to shift for obtaining the more important finger/thumb and lateral weight. Actually, top weight can stabilize or destabilize the roll of the ball prior to impact, and it can increase or decrease deflection after impact, depending upon its position at the point of impact. Problems can arise from too much top weight. I have seen the ball wobble during its travel toward the pins. Such a wobble is seen more readily with excessive numbers of revolutions and a great amount of turn at the release. This, I feel, is a misuse of top weight because the wobble interferes with the desired action and roll.

(*Author's Note:* What in modern bowling jargon is called "flair" is the oil pattern on the ball that reflects gyration, or wobble, of the axis of rotation. Although flair is being sold as beneficial, I continue to maintain that the best and most predictable ball is one wherein the axis is stable, not wobbling, before it contacts the pins.)

What is too much top weight? I really do not know. Generally, a ball with less revolutions can carry more top weight, but this is probably not a useful rule either. I use no more than two ounces because any more tends to make my ball overreact with small inconsistencies in my delivery. The possibility exists that many top weight positions are useless.

A source of error exists in top weight calculations. The manuals state that approximately 75% of the weight removed by the holes from a sixteen-pound ball is removed as top weight. (About 80% of the weight removed from a fourteen pound ball is removed as top weight.) The reason that these figures do not approach 100% is that, as the holes are drilled they usually pass the weight block center. Therefore, the deeper the hole the less it reduces the top weight. If there were no weight block and the ball were the same material all of the way throughout, the holes would remove 100% of their weight as top weight. At any rate, the depth of the weight blocks, their shape, and their densities relative to those of the core and shell contribute to this source of error. I really do not think that this approximate figure for top weight removal can ever be made more accurate.

(**Author's Note:** The way top weight is measured on a beam balance also contributes to this error.) More accuracy may not be necessary, and figures would have to be provided with each different design of ball.

The Full Roller

I would also like to have limited my discussion to semirolling balls simply because weight shift can be used to greater advantage with them. Generally, weight shifts change the spatial relationship of the track to the grip. As you can see in Figure 33, the amount of positive/negative, finger/thumb weight that can be obtained by shifting the weight center in directions D or I within a full-rolling ball (A), is limited by the chance of the track being moved over either the thumbhole or the middle fingerhole. This track results from lifting (vertical rotation) but not turning (horizontal rotation) the ball at the point of release. With the semiroller (B), as the weight center is moved in the direction of D, the track moves lower on the ball. Another way of saying this is that the axis of rotation of the ball changes in response to the weight center shift. (When we say that a track moves lower on the ball, this does not mean that the track takes on a smaller diameter. Rather, we mean that the track (hence the axis) changes angle or pitch. A smaller diameter track would result from more turn at the release.)

Figure 33: A Comparison of the Full Roller Track (A) and the Semiroller Track (B) With Respect to Weight Placement and Axis of Rotation (AR)

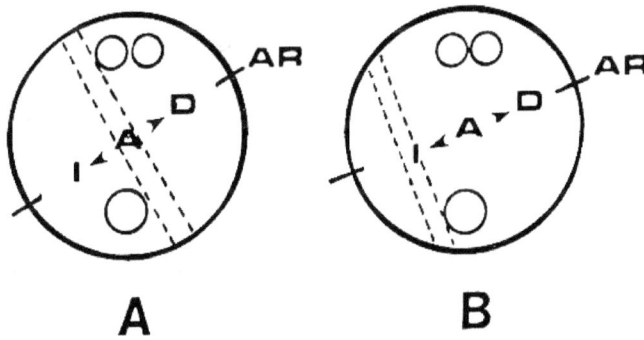

A   B

One interesting point is that some bowlers, although they turn the ball at the release, still show an almost fully circumferential track. The only difference is that the track does not pass through the grip area. In the case of full rollers, I do not know to what degree a weight shift can bring about different effects on the roll, but I believe that adaptive changes in side weight are more common than in finger/thumb weight.

The inability of the full rollers to keep pace with the semirollers in scoring potential is evident. It may be that this is simply a function of being outnumbered, but I think, more realistically, this type of ball is less adaptable to different lane conditions — especially the harder lane finishes. In the days of the soft shellac lane finish, and even into the era of the lacquer finish, full rollers were high scoring. The situation today has reversed itself, probably because the full roller skids too much before hooking, and the hook is often not powerful enough for the hard finishes. The solutions to the problems of full rollers may not be difficult, and they may be solved by differences in bowling ball design; but solutions have been elusive, and maybe the best one is for the bowler to switch to a semiroller.

Weight Block Design

There are almost infinite possibilities for weight block design, but only a small number had been employed until just a few years ago. Now, there are several designs in production, and Figure 34 presents some of these. All perspectives are the same with the top of the ball in the same position in all diagrams. Type A is the standard "puddle" design used for many years by Brunswick, AMF, Ace, Columbia, and Manhattan. It is a small, compact mass of dense material between the core and the shell. Type B is the design used in some Ebonite balls. The weight block was approximately half of the core, and I guess this could be considered one of the first deep weight blocks. Type C is the disc-shaped block seen in the Randolph Classic ball recommended for semiroller bowlers. It is a shallower block than that of Randolph's type D (a bowl or platelet shape), which is intended for the full roller bowler. Type E is included just for fun. It is a cubical block of barium encased in an acrylic ball. These balls appeared on the market in the early 1960's, and, although attractive, they never

Figure 34: Various Weight Block Designs – The stripes indicate material that is denser than the rest of the ball. Diagram H does not show a true weight block. All perspectives are the same as in diagram A.

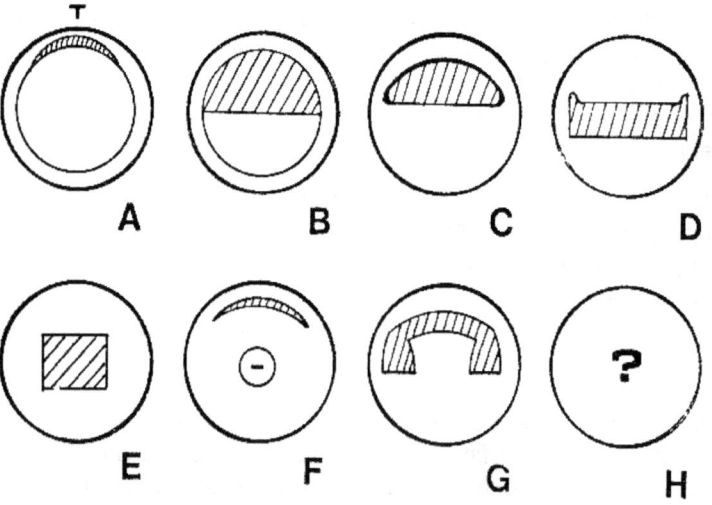

were high-scoring. The reason for the low scoring was the extreme hardness (above 90 durometric reading) of the shell. The cubical weight block was not unsuccessful, but I have never seen it used in any other ball. Type F is seen in the MSG Star Trak polyester ball.

Although the ball has a weight block, another feature has been added. The circle with a minus sign in it indicates a low density area. Type G is the telephone receiver-shaped weight block of the Amburgey ball. It supposedly exerts a positive gyroscopic effect on the roll of the ball, but I really do not know enough about this ball to give a detailed treatment. Type H is non-existent. It indicates that there are always possibilities for new designs innovated by young-thinking individuals. Why don't you physics hobbyists sit down and invent the ideal, perfect, and most effective weight block? Let me know what you come up with!

Depth of the Weight Center

Even though the punch mark is stamped on the surface of the ball to indicate the position of the weight center, it says nothing about the distance of the weight center from the geometric center (or surface). The weight center may be deep (closer to the geometric center) or shallow (closer to the surface). Figure 35 illustrates this point. In general, the deep weight center makes the ball skid less, begin an earlier roll, and hook more gradually, regardless of (reasonable) placement of the weight center. The shallow weight center makes the ball skid further, hook later, and break more abruptly; but, in this case, the placement of the weight center is critical.

Figure 35: A Comparison of Deep and Shallow Weight Centers (W) – The deep weight center is closer to the geometric center of the ball than to the surface. The opposite is true for the shallow weight center.

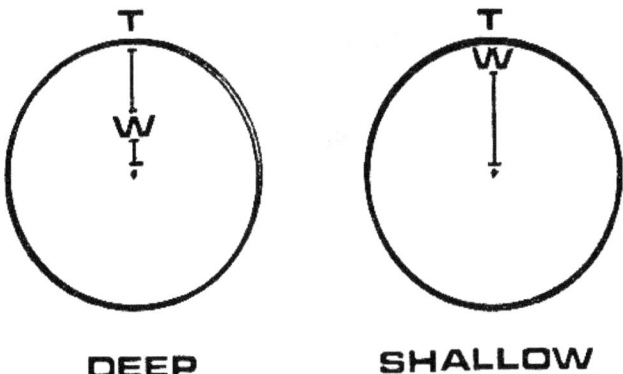

DEEP   SHALLOW

When two balls having identical weights but different weight blocks are weighed, one can often obtain similar accurate measurements.

These readings are valid statically (on a beam balance), but *dynamically (when the ball is rolling), the distance of the weight center from the geometric center becomes all-important.* On the beam balance, the influence of a given amount of weight is a function of the distance (Z), but when the ball is rolling, this influence is a function of the square of the same distance. Figure 36 shows this. Assuming we have weighed these two balls and have obtained a weight center (we will call it top weight for the sake of clarity) measurement of 2.0 ounces for both, let us present two simple cases.

Figure 36: Assigning Arbitrary Distances Between the Ball Center and the Deep (Z1) and Shallow (Z2) Weight Centers — In both cases, the top weight is two ounces.

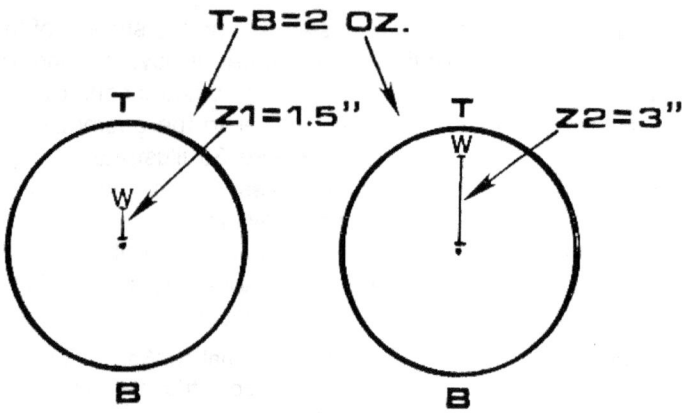

Case 1: Influence of the weight center on the balance as it is being weighed or as the ball is skidding as opposed to rolling:
Deep Weight Center 2.0 x 1.5 = 3.0
Shallow Weight Center 2.0 x 3.0 = 6.0
Result: The shallow weight center exerts twice the influence.

Case 2: Influence of the weight center on the balance as the ball is rolling:
Deep Weight Center $2.0 \times (1.5)^2 = 4.5$
Shallow Weight Center $2.0 \times (3.0)^2 = 18.0$
Result: The shallow weight center exerts four times the influence.

Of course, these cases have been oversimplified. The action of a ball on the lane is an extremely complicated interplay of friction, speed, mass, weight block shape, and other unknown factors, and physicists have puzzled for years over these phenomena. However, some useful generalities can be made. If one needs to make the most out of weights to achieve a greater hook (i.e. a more powerful ball), he should choose one with a shallow weight center. If he wants a quicker roll with a gradual hook, he should choose a deeper weight block. It is fair to tell you that manufacturers are "pushing" the shallow weight block in combination with a softer or more porous shell to fit today's lane conditions. I do not put much confidence in fads, but some of these innovations (even though they are heavily promoted) can help a bowler. To make a proper decision for yourself, get together with a reputable, skillful driller and experiment before buying an expensive, commercially attractive bowling ball.

Drilling of Extra Holes to Shift the Weight Center

This is of limited value for two reasons. The first is that some regulations will not allow more than four holes in the ball, and sometimes more than one extra hole is necessary to shift a sufficient amount of weight in the proper direction. The second, and more important, reason is that although one can measure the desired weight shift (resulting from drilling the extra hole) on the beam balance, the shape of the mass of the ball changes. The ball with additional holes will not perform dynamically the same as a similarly-weighted ball with only the grip holes. Even though it seems that the two should act the same based on the static (beam) balance, a dynamic (moving) analysis should bring out the small, but significant, differences.

Loading a Bowling Ball

This is the practice of adding denser material in certain places to give greater imbalance. The weight center will shift in the direction of the added material. The material can be barium salt, screws, buckshot, BBs, lead fishing sinkers, mercury (extremely toxic and, therefore, dangerous), etc. Obviously, this practice is unethical and against ABC regulations (if the added material is metallic and/or if the imbalance exceeds ABC limits). It is also the reason why the Professional Bowlers Association (PBA) will not allow plugged balls to be used in its tournaments. In fact, one of the cases that prompted the adoption of this restriction was one in which a bowler loaded each side of the track axis of a fourteen-pound ball with a pound of barium to create a sixteen-pound ball. It seemed legal, the imbalance being within weight tolerances as measured on a static balance.

Dynamically, the ball showed strongly advantageous pin-spilling characteristics, hence the PBA restriction on plugged balls. Now, and probably wisely, weight blocks must be put into the ball by the manufacturer only, at least as far as the PBA is concerned.

Weighing Bowling Balls

I will not include stepwise procedures for using the beam balance because I feel that these have been discussed very well in two publications. One, **General Instructions for Weighing and Balancing Bowling Balls on a Beam Scale**, is available free from ABC. The other is written by Bill Taylor and is available for a fee from Western Columbia Inc. It is entitled **Weighing a Bowling Ball for Balance and Imbalance**. Figure 37 shows a typical beam balance and a ball upon which are indicated axes of alignment for weighing.

Figure 37: A Typical Beam (Static) Balance and a Ball Showing the Axes of Measured Finger/Thumb and Lateral Weights (C is the center of the grip)

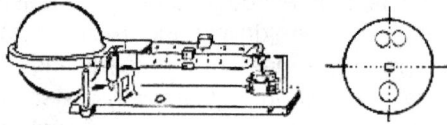

This scale is as accurate as is practical, but it is far from perfectly accurate. The machine must be absolutely level, and this is taken care of to some extent by a bubble indicator. Perhaps the biggest source of error (besides inability of the operator to understand it) is that there is usually no built-in means of properly aligning the weighing axes. If it is suspected that these axes are off by as little as 1/8 inch, the weight error can be as great as 1/8 ounce. Such a difference can mean the ball may exceed legal limits.

One Man's Meat is Another Man's Poison

The degree to which the same amount of imbalance can help either of two bowlers cannot be predicted with absolute success. Even if both bowlers roll the same track; speed, the amount of lift, and the amount of tension in the swing can influence the weights differently. Although generalizations about weight placement can be made, they are subject to limitations imposed by small differences in the delivery as well as intrinsic differences from one ball to another (core, shell, etc.). The only way in which valid conclusions can be made about the effect of weight imbalance on the roll of a particular bowler's ball will be through some sort of dynamic analysis of that ball and not through static analysis as on the beam scale. It has been known for a number of years that a better automobile tire balance can be obtained by a dynamic (moving or speed) balance than can be obtained by a static (or bubble) balance device. The same line of reasoning should apply to bowling balls.

8 Surface Properties of the Bowling Ball

Author's Note — Old vs. New: Preparation of ***Perceptive Bowling*** began in 1976 and was completed in 1979. It took an additional year for the publisher to release it to the market. Because it pre-dates urethane balls, this book contains no information relating specifically to "reactive resin" urethane balls or to those with high-traction particles embedded in the covers.

Particle urethane balls did not appear until the early 1980's, when Brunswick introduced the red Edge. This was revolutionary and very effective on heavily-oiled lane surfaces. It had extremely high-traction qualities similar to the contemporary Brunswick LT-48 rubber balls (which had ground walnut shells in the cover) and the mica particle-embedded urethane balls of today. The Edge would still be an effective ball on modern synthetic lane surfaces.

Reactive resin balls did not appear until the early 1990's, with introduction of the Nu-Line Excaliber. This ball slid further on oil and hooked more on the dry portions of the lane than the non-resin urethane AMF Angle or the Hammer, popular at the time. It remains a useful ball on today's lane conditions.

Modern urethane balls perform similarly to older high-tech counterparts introduced to the market before 1980, such as the Columbia Yellow Dot soft polyester ball and the Ebonite Magnum 10 soft rubber ball. In its day, the Yellow Dot "bleeder" ball was a wildly high-scoring ball that was most effective on hooking and blocked lane surfaces.

Therefore, this chapter is historically informative and is still of value to the modern-day bowler. I suggest that you read this material, keeping in mind that much of the information is useful in understanding surface properties of modern bowling balls.)

Hardness

The surface properties of the bowling ball have in recent years become one of the most controversial issues that the sport has experienced. Most of this controversy stems from the practice on the PBA tour a few years ago of soaking polyester balls in methyl ethyl ketone (MEK), an acetone-related organic solvent that can soften the cover or shell. This was done to overcome the slicker lane conditions brought about by the application of oil to the newer plastic lane finishes. Known as "soakers," these balls were eventually prohibited by both the PBA and ABC. One professional used these soakers to great success to become the bowler of the year, and his performance prompted many others to follow suit and become fellow soakers.

As the popularity of the softer-shelled balls grew, manufacturers answered the demand by offering both rubber and plastic balls with durometric hardnesses sometimes below 60. Balls with this low hardness reading are so soft that the fingernail can make an indentation on the cover. Therefore, the softer the ball, the more of the surface contacts the lane surface at any instant. Bowling is a game of millimeters, and the difference in the width of the contact area of a softer ball (as opposed to a harder ball) may be small, but it is significant enough to make a great difference in the hooking action. Unfortunately, the soft balls do not hold up to the stresses of the bowling game, and they wear down quickly. Further, even though scoring can be terrifically high with them, the soft balls are not suited to a wide variety of lane conditions — especially the slower or hooking lanes.

Presently, companies manufacture balls with a lower limit of 72 in mind, and only occasionally does a ball softer than that appear in the retail store. The PBA has imposed a lower limit of 75 durometric hardness. In the interim period between the time of manufacture and distribution of the less-than-72 balls and that of the imposition of the regulations, many bowlers and retailers were left literally holding the bag (or, more correctly, the ball). Many bowlers who were previously unable to adapt their deliveries and other equipment to some lane conditions were indeed able to use the softer balls to great advantage to produce higher scores. The softer balls may still be used in unsanctioned tournaments that have adopted no hardness rules (although some other participants may be violently opposed to their use, but only those balls harder than the lower limit may be used in tournaments sanctioned by the ABC or conducted by the PBA.

There are many problems involved in enforcing bowling ball hardness regulations. I believe that such rules can, after a fashion, be enforced only if strict standardization of the measuring devices and parameters) is accomplished. If the enforcement of regulations is to be completely fair, the tests of hardness must be reliable. That is, the hardness of the ball must read the same (within narrow limits of error) on every test instrument of the same make and model. The regulations concerning hardness must be further clarified by basing the lower limit on exacting margins of error and at a standard hardness temperature. Instead of the lower limit reading "72 durometer hardness", it should read, "72 + or – 0.5 Rex (or Shore) D hardness at a temperature of — degrees F (or C)."

To achieve this level of accuracy, two essential standardizations can be made at the time of the test. On-the-spot calibration of the test instrument can be accomplished by testing the hardness of a standard bar of metal, the hardness of which is known at the ambient temperature of the test found on a chart provided with the test bar by the manufacturer). The temperature of the ball can never be measured accurately, but a working estimate can be made by the following simple method. A rubber stopper with a thermometer pushed through it is inserted snugly into one of the holes in the ball. The sensing tip should be a predetermined depth into the hole — an inch, for example. The ball, with thermometer in place, should be allowed to equilibrate for a few minutes until the temperature does not change appreciably. The hardness of the ball can then be measured by a calibrated instrument, the reading stated in terms of the temperature measured by the thermometer in the ball. The governing body will have decided, before the test was made and regardless of who measured the hardness, whether or not to allow the measured hardness of the ball at the measured temperature. Of course, this would necessitate the promulgation of a chart that shows allowable hardnesses at measured temperatures, but it is the only fair, equitable method. It is my strong feeling that the ability to impose restrictions obligates the rulemaking body to precisely define the rules under which the restrictions are made. Otherwise, rules will always be unfair and unenforceable, and bad feelings will result.

The problems involved in measurement may be too great to solve with the expertise of the personnel involved. Also, the value (durability vs. cost) of the softer balls may not be important to the bowler. At any rate, the decision of restricting the hardness or softness of the bowling ball must be made with the consumer in mind, and I have serious reservations about any organization being able to make the decision in a totally objective manner.

Porosity

Porosity, or the number of pores within a given area of the surface, is another way in which the amount of hooking action is regulated. This is a characteristic more commonly seen in rubber balls. The depth, size, and number per square unit area are varied to allow for more or less grab on the lane surface. Obviously, the more pores per square inch (or centimeter), the more traction the ball will have on the lane.

Scratches

Another characteristic that can be varied is the number of scratches that are put on the cover. One can take fine or medium fine sandpaper and sand the entire surface of the ball to produce a dull finish. Then, a little white (aluminum oxide) or red (iron oxide) rubbing compound can be applied to give a little shine. The deeper scratches will remain on the surface, and the shine will make the ball appear to be smooth. Of course, the more scratches, the greater the hook. Care must be taken, however, not to put excessively deep scratches on the ball and not to sand only the track lest the ball not pass ABC inspection.

Pigment in the Shell

Another factor to be considered is the type of pigment used in the cover. For years, better bowlers knew that colored rubber balls tended to have a crustier texture than black ones. The old Brunswick Fireball and Starfire, the Ebonite Emerald 300, and the Manhattan "Green Pea" (at least, that's what I always have heard it called) are good examples. Further, in the first years of the PBA tour, regular players began to use polyester balls. Many of these bowlers believed that the Columbia 300 Caramel ball had a higher-traction texture. Of course, no one could verify this notion with the manufacturer, and now one sees all colors being used with regularity.

Cleanliness of the Ball

This point is one that, I feel, will increase in importance with continued use of the more viscous (heavier) oils suited for the plastic lane finishes. I have found that a complete degreasing of the ball before each delivery gives a better finish and more positive roll to the ball. This holds true for both plastic and rubber balls, and the idea makes sense because, in truth, the ball is designed so that the cover contacts the lane. Since oil and dirt are inseparable, these combine to produce a film on the ball, and this film can transfer easily to the fingers. Thus, oil and dirt present a twofold problem — less traction on the lane and less security of the grip on the ball. This is why I degrease the ball (while bowling on something other than dry and hooking lanes) before every delivery and why I degrease the holes often.

In the old days, bowlers used rubbing alcohol, lighter fluid, or some other dangerous volatile solvent to clean the ball, but, with the advent of the polyester ball, it was found that these could affect the cover (softening, glazing, etc.) and also leave an oil-solvent residue that was slimier than the original oil. It is against ABC regulations to use these volatile solvents on the ball (remember the "soakers") so I have searched for a water-based degreaser that leaves no residue, that evaporates quickly, that does not dry the hands (remove the natural oils) and that can be used while bowling. I believe I have found the ideal substance, Shaklee Corporation's Basic H. A mixture (two tablespoons of Basic H to a pint of water) applied to a towel can be used to wipe the ball before each delivery. It can be used on the hands as well, and after bowling, a simple rinsing with water will completely clean off all remaining degreaser. Remember, oil and dirt are the bowler's worst enemy. Oil should be used generously on the lanes, but when the ball picks it up, it can eventually get onto the hands. Try the degreasing method; I think it can help you.

Quality Control

I should end this chapter by trying to give you a chart that tells exactly which balls have which characteristics, but the truth is that quality control problems in the production of these balls makes it almost impossible for one to generalize about shell or cover characteristics. It is not the fault of the manufacturer when he produces a ball that is hard when it should be soft. It is, however, his and the retailer's fault when they misrepresent the product. Every company claims to offer different hardnesses in both rubber and polyester balls, and you can find this out by calling a dealer. However, if you want an exact hardness measurement of a ball, it must be tested by an accurate durometer. Only then can you be assured of the hardness, and even this may change with time, use, and means of storage.

9 Increasing Your Adaptive Range

Have you ever wondered why you struggle so much to bowl your average one week and are beating the pins to death the next? Have you envied the bowler who never seems to have a really low series and is consistently high-scoring in almost every establishment? The chances are that you may not have learned how to increase your adaptive range. The consistent bowler seems to squeeze every bit of scoring potential out of any set of lane conditions he encounters. Most likely, both of you know how to make changes in speed and angle of attack in efforts to suit the conditions. But further, he may have been able to utilize one or more of the characteristics we have been discussing in the previous chapters. I myself was afraid to use a plastic ball for 18 years of bowling, and I did not really concern myself with bowling ball hardness and weight distribution until my twelfth year of bowling. I feel that I would have been a better bowler much sooner if I had been more receptive to change. I do not advocate a wholesale change to a plastic ball, rather I believe one should use variations of any reasonable characteristic to accomplish the betterment of his score. In short, one must have what I call a Bag of Shots to confront different lane situations appropriately.

In this chapter, I give you some more specific information necessary for you to cope with various lane conditions. It is the logical extension of the skills discussed in chapter six, **Bowling Geometrics**. It Is a compilation of my 20 years of experience but it includes more than just what I do when I am playing lanes. Obviously, any individual is limited as to how much he can change his game to adjust to the conditions at hand, and just telling you what I do would be only part of the picture. Consequently, I have gathered facts from numerous sources, many of which I cannot even remember. Much of the information is common knowledge but never has been put into a single work before. My original contributions in this chapter are the commentary on each of the lane conditions, the assignment of priorities to the possible solutions based on their value in solving the problems, and an evaluation of the solutions based on their degree of interference with good bowling form.

The Problem and Solution in Terms of Goals

When playing a lane, we are trying to solve (adapt to) an immediate problem (the lane conditions) in the quickest way possible. Another way of saying this is that our objective is to find the proper combination of factors that let us consistently hit the pocket and carry the pins. This is more than just hitting the headpin and avoiding splits. Sometimes we are just not able to accomplish this objective no matter what we do, and this brings to mind one of my greatest criticisms of bowling instruction manuals — they don't tell you that there are some lane conditions on which acceptable scoring is impossible. Some lane conditions are lousy, and we might as well admit it! A more subtle way of saying this is that the scoring potential of the lane is low, or more correctly, that the scoring potential of the lane is outside the adaptive range of most, if not all, bowlers. I suppose the authors feel that the bowler would give up trying to master the lane, or that he will use the lane conditions as an excuse for poor performance. I must give the bowler more credit than that! Maybe a dog would give up trying to get a dish of food beyond his reach, but a bowler in pursuit of good scores is different. The competitive spirit and the ego come into the picture, and I feel that most bowlers honestly try to play the lanes no matter how low the scoring potential.

Surely, one cannot bowl well on all conditions all of the time, but there are some intelligent ways in which a person can keep from scoring too badly. In the long run, the highest averages are not usually held by the bowlers who bowl the highest single scores. Granted, high averagers are the ones who bowl high scores when conditions are good, but they are also the ones who do not bowl such low scores when conditions are bad. Your overall goal is not to bowl well. This is not properly defined. It is a hazy goal, and you cannot achieve a goal that you do not clearly understand. Rather, most of the time, you should set your sights on bowling, high scores in relation to the scoring potential of the lane you are bowling on at the time. You cannot accomplish the hazy goal, but you can attain the well-defined goal with success. Think of the frustration you would experience if you could not bowl expected high scores on poor lanes. Frustration is followed by anger, and anger is the most common cause of a lack of concentration, hence the downward spiral effect.

The solutions to the lane condition problems that I present are not to be taken as prescriptions. I cannot tell you what you are capable of doing. They are to be considered as general directions that are available to you. You may or may not be able to use all of them; in fact, you may be able to devise new directions of your own. I feel that, If I give you sufficient information, you can make intelligent decisions for yourself. I can tell you some effects of alterations in bowling ball characteristics and in the delivery, but you must apply these variations to your own game. Further, you must learn yourself (know what you are capable of) so well that the adjustment to a certain lane condition can be made quickly. Time passes very fast in a league session or tournament; time is money, and every frame bowled incorrectly can be costly.

Any one of the strategies that I discuss has its limitation of usefulness, and combinations of many strategies can be used at the discretion of the bowler. Only through practice on many different lane conditions, combined with a desire for self-improvement, concentration, and self-confidence that you can try many different techniques can you hope to increase your adaptive range. There is success in failure; likewise, no one ever learned from never bowling badly; so never be afraid to try something new. Jim St. John won the World's Invitational Tournament by moving to the unheard of second-board strike angle. He easily outdistanced the field. Why? Because he wasn't afraid to change — even when the change could have cost him a place in the finals. Such bravery! Follow his example! Remember that he had an effective adaptive range. Do you?

What is an Intelligent Decision?

I think I can best answer this question by the following situation. Assume, in choosing a bowling ball, that:

1. There are only 24 categories of ball hardness (only whole number durometer readings from 72 through 96). (24)
2. You may choose either a polyester or a rubber cover. (2)
3. You may select either 3, 2, or 1 ounces of top weight. (3)

4. You may have only 1 ounce of either positive or negative lateral weight. (2)
5. You may choose only 1 ounce of either finger or thumb weight. (2)

Mathematically, the possible combinations of the above choices (the numbers in parentheses) that can appear in one bowling ball are:

$$24 \times 2 \times 3 \times 2 \times 2 = 576.$$

This means that, to obtain bowling balls with every possible combination of the five parameters listed above, one would have to purchase 576 balls! These combinations do not reflect all of the choices; the combinations are infinite. One may choose half-numbers on the hardness scale, an acrylic cover, 1/8-ounce increments in top/bottom, lateral, and finger/thumb weight, or a different type of core. Also left to consider are the effects of hand position, hole pitches, speed of the swing, etc.

It must be apparent by now that you have a tremendous number of options available. What decisions will you make to be most adaptable for the least outlay of money for equipment and practice? This is a highly individual problem, and no one can tell you exactly what to do in this or any other book. Once you have finished reading this book, I hope you can make these decisions in a manner that is based on sound reasoning.

Variable Characteristics – A Pep Talk

In a previous section, I spoke of the "variation of any reasonable characteristic" to accomplish better scoring. Further, I said one must have a "bag of shots" to be fully adaptable. Well, you may ask, "What is a characteristic?" Or, better yet, you may wonder, "What is a reasonable one?" A reasonable characteristic, in my opinion, is one that may be varied without interfering with the basic essentials of the delivery. For example, one would not think of changing the angle of the swing relative to the body plane to play a certain lane; this would be unreasonable, and no good instructor would advise this variation, since a straight swing is one of the essentials to consistent bowling.

How does a bowler develop the use of a characteristic into a method that lets him adapt to a wide range of lane conditions? Consider

Figure 38, a flow chart that illustrates a very complex thought/action process in a very simple, diagrammatic way.

Figure 38: The Process of Increasing Adaptive Range (collecting a bag of shots)

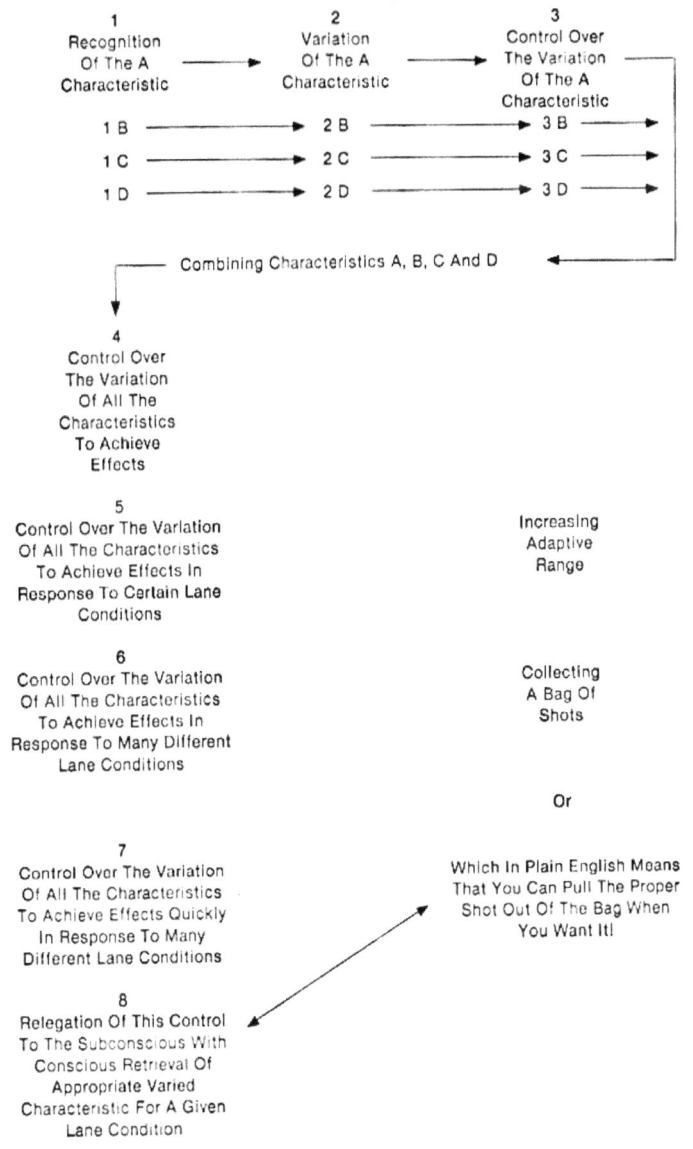

When a bowler discovers a characteristic, I like to say that he has recognized it (1). That is, he exhibited the characteristic (for example, holding his wrist in the fully extended, 180-degree position) before he recognized it Let's call this characteristic A. The same recognition process takes place with other characteristics at the same time; let's call of these B, C, and D. With the passage of time, development of muscle balance, and intelligent practice, the bowler's ability increases to the point where he can vary the characteristic (2). With more practice and additional knowledge he discovers that he can exercise some control over the characteristic (as with A, he can change the degree of flexion of the wrist at the release) (3). With more practice the bowler can learn to control the variation to achieve noticeable effects on a lane (4). The same process has occurred with characteristics B, C, and D, so that, from this stage on, they may develop in combination with A. The next step (5) is the ability of the bowler to control the variation of the characteristics to achieve effects in response to certain lane conditions. Next, he develops the ability to employ these variations on many lane conditions (6) until he can eventually adapt quickly (7). The last three steps (5, 6, and 7) involve higher-level conditioning, and more ability is required because the effects must be tested on different lane conditions.

Naturally, the highest level is that of making quick variations when confronted with a particular lane condition (8). This may be more than can be hoped for, but it is certainly a desirable goal. The last three, and probably four, steps also encompass what I have been calling *increasing one's adaptive range*, and I guess you can see that it probably involves more than can be understood by any human being. Do not give up hope, however! **One does not have to understand everything, about a process to use it.** All you need to know is that it works; I and all you need to do is recognize some variables to be on your way!

The delivery, as I have mentioned before, is composed of many different characteristics. Some of these can be varied without interfering with the coordination, balance, and timing; some cannot be varied without such interference. **The following is a list of characteristics that I recommend should never be used as adaptive variables under any circumstances.** You should not change these to play a particular lane condition.

1. *The proper leverage positions (timing) throughout the delivery.*

2. The *proper alignment of all planes* as explained in the chapter devoted to the release.
3. *The followthrough should always be the same speed as the downswing.* No matter if the downswing is of constant speed or is accelerated, there should be no abrupt change in this speed at the point of release. Therefore, a constant relationship should exist between the speed of the swing and the amount of lift. The faster the downswing, the stronger the lift (see calculation of F in chapter five).
4. *The thumb clears the thumbhole cleanly, and the fingers squeeze at the release.* Therefore, a chance is given for good leverage each and every release.
5. *The speed of the footwork matches the length of the swing.* The longer the swing, the slower the footwork; the shorter the swing, the faster the footwork. Therefore, variation of the speed of the footwork (cadence) is not really decided to a great degree by the bowler. It is, rather, dependent upon the length of the swing, the starting position of the stance, and the length of the approach. The starting position should be determined by the number of steps and the length of the stride, and these are relatively constant.

These five characteristics are what authors call "good habits," and, if you haven't already noticed, **these are the characteristics that serious bowlers sharpen through constant practice to keep them consistent, i.e. unvaried!** Likewise, the serious bowler does not and should not practice the variable characteristics with the aim of keeping them consistent. However, he should **practice them with the objective of learning how much he can vary them and of observing what their variance does to the roll of the ball on a given lane.**

What are some of the characteristics that a bowler may safely use as adaptive variables? My answer to this is the ones that affect the roll of the ball without interfering with the delivery. After taking stock of many characteristics of the delivery and deciding the ones necessary for maintenance of good form, I found that very few were left that could safely be varied. However, **the list that follows probably includes the only ones necessary for a bowler to have a good amount of adaptability.** You may be able to recognize some more, but I think that you will at least agree with these.

1. **Variation of the amount of flexion/extension of the hand at the wrist** *(Figure 39, A)*. An extension of the wrist to the 180-degree position results in what I term maximum V, and changing the hand from this position is what I call "*changing V.*" At the 180 degree position, the vertical distance (V) between the base of the thumb and the lifting pads of the fingers is the greatest. This allows for the greatest amount of lift (vertical rotation) of the ball at the release. Decreasing V gives the ball more skid and a later hook. A full back extension of the wrist gives minimum V, the most skid, and the least amount of hook of all of the flexion/extension positions.

2. *Variation of the position of the thumb at the release with the position held throughout the swing and release (Figure 39, B)*. Theoretically; as the thumb is moved from the 9:00 o'clock position to the 2:00 o'clock position through successive deliveries, one position per delivery (changing Th); one should expect less hook. Less hook usually means less power on the ball, but this is not strictly true. Some lane conditions favor a rolling ball, and at the later clockface numbers, one may actually see a stronger rolling ball even with a smaller hook. I would like to point out that a 12:00 o'clock thumb, normally accepted to be the standard for the straight ball, often results in either a hook or a reverse hook (backup ball) because of the pitch relationship of the thumb to the fingers (Figure 39, B, second diagram). Since this terminology is standardized, I will not challenge its meaning. However, I suggest that when you think of varying the position of the thumb, you should also consider the position of the fingers relative to the thumb and to each other at the release.

3. *Variation of the position of the thumb with turn (horizontal rotation) imparted by the fingers at the release (changing Th with turn)*. The starting positions of the thumb are still as shown in Figure 39, B, but as the hand passes the foot in the slide, the wrist is turned so that the thumb returns to the 9:00 o'clock position at the release. More precisely, the turn is imparted in the short time period during the exit of the thumb and after the thumb has cleared the thumbhole; the lift ends this time period. In other words, this time interval is marked by

the beginning of the release of the thumb and the clearing of the holes by the fingers. It is a short instant indeed!

Figure 39: Variable Hand Positions

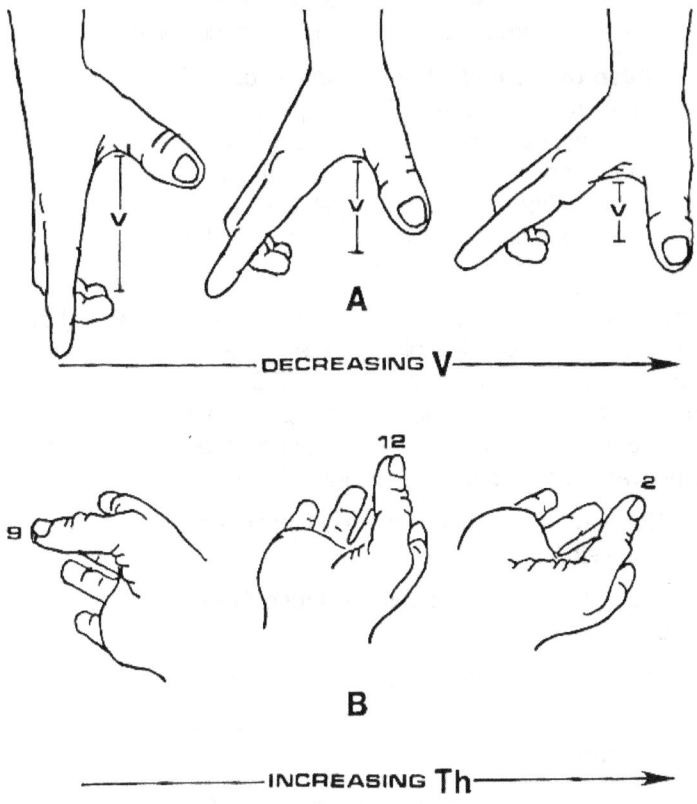

More horizontal rotation brings about more skid and a later hook, but, since more revolutions are imparted than with the straight (held thumb position) lift, the hook may be greater, depending on the speed of the ball. This is probably why the lift-and-turn release is being seen more frequently on the new lane conditions.

4. *Variation in the point of release.* This should not be varied by changing the timing relationship between the swing and the footwork, because the balance points of the entire delivery can change. The earlier release should be one in which the ball contacts the lane only a few inches (5" – 10") beyond the foul

line. This makes the ball skid less and roll earlier, and this can be an advantage on an oily lane. Putting the ball farther beyond the foul line (1' -2') can be accomplished by bending the knees more and holding on to the ball a split second longer. Ideally, the ball should be released on the upswing, but some lane and approach conditions do not encourage this.

5. *Speed of the ball.* This variable is controlled by the length of the swing, but quite a bit of speed can be generated by a bowler with a short swing if his footwork is faster. Forward ball speed can also be slightly increased the more the thumb position aligns with the target line (more toward the 12:00 o'clock position). The direction of lift is parallel with the direction of the ball, therefore, forward speed is added.

Do you remember the illustration of the number of bowling balls one would have to buy to obtain the possible combinations of characteristics? I arrived at a figure of 576 balls even when I limited the number of possible variables! Let's perform the same analysis on the variable characteristics of the delivery and limit the number of possible variations in a similar fashion. Assume that:

1. The bowler can hold only three flexion/extension positions. (3 possibilities)

2. The only thumb positions are those from 9:00 through 2:00 in one-hour increments. (6)

3. The bowler can hold or turn the wrist position. (2)

4. The bowler can place the ball only five or twelve inches past the foul line. (2)

5. The bowler can successfully employ only three ball speeds. (3)

Mathematically, the number of possible combinations of these variations is:

$$3 \times 6 \times 2 \times 2 \times 3 = 216.$$

That is, there are 216 different combinations of five different delivery variables that a bowler can possibly achieve. Combining this with the mathematical possibilities of a limited amount of bowling ball characteristics, we obtain:

$$216 \times 576 = 124,416!$$

Therefore, this bowler has a bag of shots containing 124,416 different shots or roll characteristics that he can use in conjunction with different target lines to hit the pocket and carry the pins, but... hey, wait a minute! Do I mean that he has to carry 576 bowling balls around with him wherever he goes to bowl? Am I saying that he has to master 216 different types of delivery? Absolutely not! A more realistic objective is necessary. First, a good bowler usually carries two bowling balls to the establishment — one rubber ball and one plastic ball, each of different surface properties and/or weight distribution. This further limits the number of useful shots to:

$$216 \times 2 = 432.$$

This figure would represent maximum flexibility (adaptability) of a bowler having two bowling balls available for use on a particular lane, the number of *useful* shots becoming smaller and more workable. Normally, a good bowler will attempt to change his target line (play a different angle) *before* he tries to change any of the aforementioned characteristics in the delivery. However, when different angles fail, he must be able to use a good number of the delivery variables to hit and carry the pins. A good number is the number of characteristics he can successfully vary — i.e. the ones that he can vary without interfering with his delivery. Of his 432 shots, some are so similar that they are essentially the same, so the bowler will generalize them and use fewer and fewer as his experience increases. In fact, because he may not be capable of varying all of them; he may prefer to rely on only two or three of the variables while keeping the others constant.

The bag of shots contains many combinations of characteristics assembled because of their usefulness in appropriate situations. This is where you come in! You, as a perceptive bowler, must choose, as soon as possible after your first delivery, the proper shot for a particular condition. If a shot is not useful on this condition, you must systematically try another one and still another one if necessary. You must know what is in your bag of shots; you must know what you can and cannot do. If you find that you cannot adapt to a certain lane, you can either pass it off and struggle, or you can try harder to work out a combination that lets you to adapt. The shot can then be put into the bag for use with a similar lane condition later. Only experience can help you develop the bag of shots; and, naturally, the more shots you develop, the quicker and more effective your adaptation to a lane will be. I can help you to a certain extent in getting you on your way to building an effective adaptive range, but you will never stop learning. You must be perceptive because you will always encounter new situations of lane conditions to which you may or may not be able to adapt. As you read the rest of this chapter, please make an extra effort to visualize what I am trying to explain. This helps to start the questioning process so necessary to your own intellectual growth.

Problems and Possible Quick Solutions

In this section, I present several common (and, therefore generalized) lane conditions, make highly-opinionated comments about each one, and tell you (if you do not yet know) how the ball reacts on the condition with reference to the particular target line employed. Then I suggest to you some alternatives that may help you quickly adapt to that condition without having to "fish around" for a shot. These alternatives use the variable characteristics of Figure 39, Table 3, and Table 4 in conjunction with various target lines. Take a few minutes to study Table 3 and Table 4, so that the information can be easily recalled as you read about the different lane conditions. Keep in mind that characteristics of the delivery should not be varied if you are able to hit the pocket and carry the pins with what you consider your most comfortable target line and shot. As your ability grows through experience, more shots will be comfortable, and you will be able to use several with equal skill. Remember, comfort and confidence (assuming you have a perfectly-fitted grip) first, then, if the shot must be changed, keep in mind the following:

1. If your comfortable shot (the one developed with your favorite target line, ball and delivery on your home lanes) does not work, change your target line. You must hit the pocket at all costs, regardless of a low strike-carrying percentage.

2. If your shot is not carrying the pins, make minor adjustments to the target line before changing any other variable. I suggest that line adjustments be made roughly according to the sequence shown in the fourth diagram of Figure 38 (A first, B second, C next and D last) — in other words, use a system.

3. If the ball still does not carry, analyze the type of leaves or ways in which pins are left standing.

   a. If there is a predominance of strong leaves (4, 4-9, 9, 4-7 and strong 10 (the 6 pin flies around the neck of the 10 pin, also called a ringing 10), find a combination of speed and hand positions that keep the ball from hooking so strongly. That is, try to lessen the angle and momentum of the ball impact.

b. If there is a predominance of weak leaves (5, 5-7, 5-10, weak 8, 8-10 and weak 10 (the 6 pin lazily drops off into the channel), then you must find a combination of speed and hand positions that increase the angle and momentum of the attack to the pocket — make the ball hook more and later, if possible.

4. If you are hitting and carrying, stay put!

5. If you are hitting but begin not to carry, check your speed. You may be getting tired and unconsciously slowing down, or you may be filled with enthusiasm and are rolling the ball harder.

6. If you are not hitting the pocket often but are carrying when you do, the chances are that your target line is appropriate but some other characteristic is inconsistent.

7. If you are hitting and carrying but, all of a sudden, the ball begins to hook too much, check yourself for overturn and excessive lift. If these are correct, then change the target line slightly. The reason for this is that the oil may be moving away (toward the pins) with successive deliveries, resulting in more traction in your track area. This happens very often and must be compensated for even during the course of a three-game league session. It is usually called breaking down of the condition in the target line area.

8. If you are hitting and carrying but begin to pull up short (the ball is not hooking sufficiently to hit the pocket squarely), check your timing, because leverage is being lost at some point. Do not change your target line; many bowlers do in this situation, but it usually can be attributed to some problem in timing.

Table 3: A Review of the Variable Characteristics of a Bowling Ball – The spans and hole sizes as well as the size of the ball are not variable.

Bowling Ball Variables	Range
Type of Cover	Rubber, plastic, acrylic
Hardness	72.?(ABC), 75.?(PBA)
Porosity or Scratches	Few and small to many and large; no quantitative estimate
Cleanliness	Oily to clean (free from oil and dirt)
Total Weight	10 -16 pounds; only 14 pounds and over is effective for better bowlers.
Top Weight	3 oz. bottom weight to 3 oz. top weight
Finger/Thumb Weight	1 oz. finger weight to 1 oz. thumb weight
Lateral Weight	1 oz. of negative weight to 1 oz. positive weight
Hole Pitches	No actual limit; limited by usefulness of a given pitch
Core Type	Less dense to dense
Depth of Weight Center	Deep (closer to the geometric center of the ball) to shallow (closer to the surface)

Table 4: Effects of Changing Certain Variables on the Action of the Ball on an Ideal Lane Condition.

Variable Characteristics (Fourteen)	Potential Effects of the Variable Characteristics on the Action of the Ball on an Ideal Lane Condition
Changing V	As the wrist is flexed from the back extended position; more lift can be imparted, resulting in an earlier roll (less skid) and a greater hook.
Changing Th Position Held	As the thumb is moved from the 9:00 to the 2:00 position; more forward roll can be imparted as opposed to side roll. Less hook results, and slight additional forward speed is generated

Table 4: Effects of Changing Certain Variables on the Action of the Ball on an Ideal Lane Condition.

Changing Th With Turn	The higher the starting position in terms of time (2:00 is later, or higher, than 9:00), the more revolutions that can be imparted. A later hook results from more skid, but a greater hook may also result because of inability to separate a strong turn from a strong lift.
Changing The Release Point	An earlier release gives an earlier hook; it may or may not give more hook depending on the lane condition, the amount of lift, and the amount of turn.
Changing The Ball Speed	A faster ball usually hooks less, but sometimes more lift results from more speed in the downswing.
Type of Cover	A plastic ball skids further and hooks more than a rubber ball of the same hardness. An acrylic ball hooks the least of the three.
Hardness of the Cover	A softer ball hooks more and earlier than a harder ball of the same cover composition.
Porosity or Scratches	A more porous or scratched surface of the cover gives greater traction and more hook.
Cleanliness of the Cover	A clean ball has greater traction on the lane and gives more hook.
Total Weight	A lighter ball (14 pounds) hooks more and later due to a longer skid. A heavier ball (16 pounds) rolls sooner but has greater momentum than a lighter ball.
Finger/Thumb Weight	Finger weight makes the ball skid further and hook later than thumb weight. Thumb weight makes the ball roll sooner and hook more gradually.
Lateral Weight	Positive lateral (side) weight makes the ball hook more, and negative lateral weight makes the ball hook less.
Fingerhole Pitch	Forward pitch gives more lift. Too much may overstretch the span.
Thumbhole Pitch	Reverse pitch gives a faster release. Too much may reduces grip security.
Type of Core	A less dense core keeps the pins down after impact relative to the denser core.
Depth of Weight Center	A deep weight center ball rolls sooner and hooks more gradually. A shallow weight center ball skids further and hooks later.

Before we can begin to consider individual cases of adaptation, some more terms are necessary. Figure 40 shows a section of lane at the level of the arrows, but now are shown the various target line terminologies, from extreme inside to extreme outside. Their relationship to the arrows and the numbers of the boards in which the arrows are imbedded is seen in the diagram. Two comments regarding these target lines are in order. First, if one directs his ball on a line from one area to another (from inside to outside, for example), his line is still named according to the position of the ball at the level of the arrows. If the ball rolls over the third arrow and then travels out to the ninth board before it starts to hook, the target line is still said to be an inside line. The second comment is that,

Figure 40: The Bowling Lane at the Level of the Arrows – The numbers indicate the board in which the arrow is imbedded (counting from the channel inward). EO = extreme outside line, O = outside line, I = inside line, and EI = extreme inside line

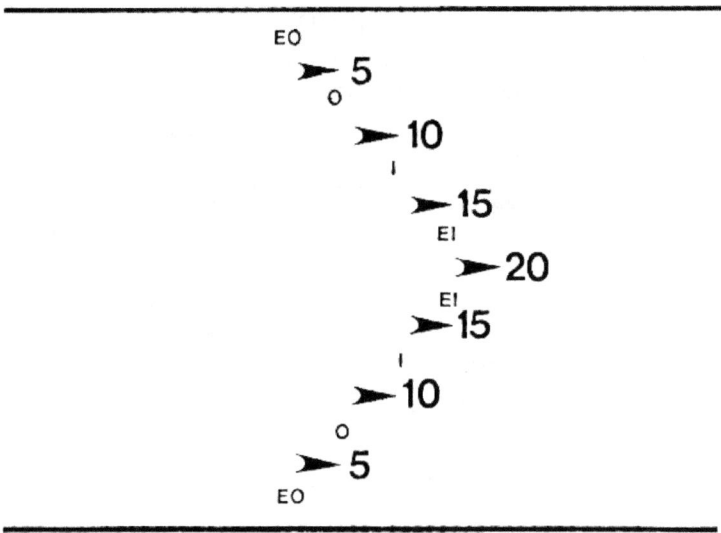

although a bowler sets his eyes on a particular target, he probably does not hit it even when the ball strikes the pocket (or pin) perfectly. If his target is the second arrow (tenth board), he probably is actually rolling the ball over the twelfth board. The reasons for this involve the fact that normal individuals have stereoscopic vision, that the eyes cannot align with the swing (unless one's head is directly over his bowling arm), and that, when the hand is aligned with the target, the tracking area on the ball may be actually a couple of inches inside the target line. A bowler may swear that he is rolling his ball over a certain board even though he is inside it. This is a normal occurrence, and it should never be the basis for strong disagreement (I have seen it happen)!

Next, I discuss the various lane conditions, all of which are shown in Figure 41 and Figure 42. The shading indicates low traction areas due to the application of dressing or oil, as it is commonly called. *The darker the shading, the lower the traction and the greater amount of dressing. The lighter the shading, the greater the traction and the lesser amount of dressing. No shading (white) indicates a high traction area devoid of oil dressing.*

Case 1: The Ideal Lane Condition

Many bowlers endlessly criticize lane conditions without offering any suggestion as to what their concept of the ideal may be. They probably have not formed an opinion. I have, however, formed a definite opinion, and I propose it to you. I feel that the best lane condition is one that allows sufficient skid before the ball rolls so that the ball reaches the target before hooking. The roll distance is sufficient for the ball to have completely overcome the skid and to have attained a complete roll so that the weight imbalance can exert its influence gradually. The dry or hooking area should allow the ball to hook gradually without deviation. The pin deck allows for minimal deflection of the ball with the pins toppling, not sliding horizontally, as they are hit. This ideal lane should let the bowler hit the pocket and carry the pins consistently from almost any angle. Very often, conditions permit only one or two playing angles, and these are usually not the ones that carry the pins effectively. Consequently, the scoring potential of the lane will remain low even if the pocket is hit consistently. On the ideal lane, the oil is densest in the head area closest to the foul line and gradually tapers or lessens to an absence of oil in the area closest to and including the pin decks. The oil never moves toward the pins and away from the original areas of application on the ideal lane. The dressing remains where it was originally applied regardless of the number of deliveries. The main point is that every bowler has a successful shot to the pocket at all times during the day. Unfortunately, this ideal lane condition is non-existent, but a lacquered lane with cross-buffed dressing came the closest to this ideal, and a freshly-dressed hard plastic lane finish can

143

come close until the oil begins, with successive deliveries of the ball, to travel toward the pins. Lacquer and the softer plastic lane finishes such as Celucoat and Thermosafe have fallen into disuse, supposedly because of the lessening of the chances of fire and less frequent refinishings with the harder finishes.

Figure 41: Four Common lane Conditions

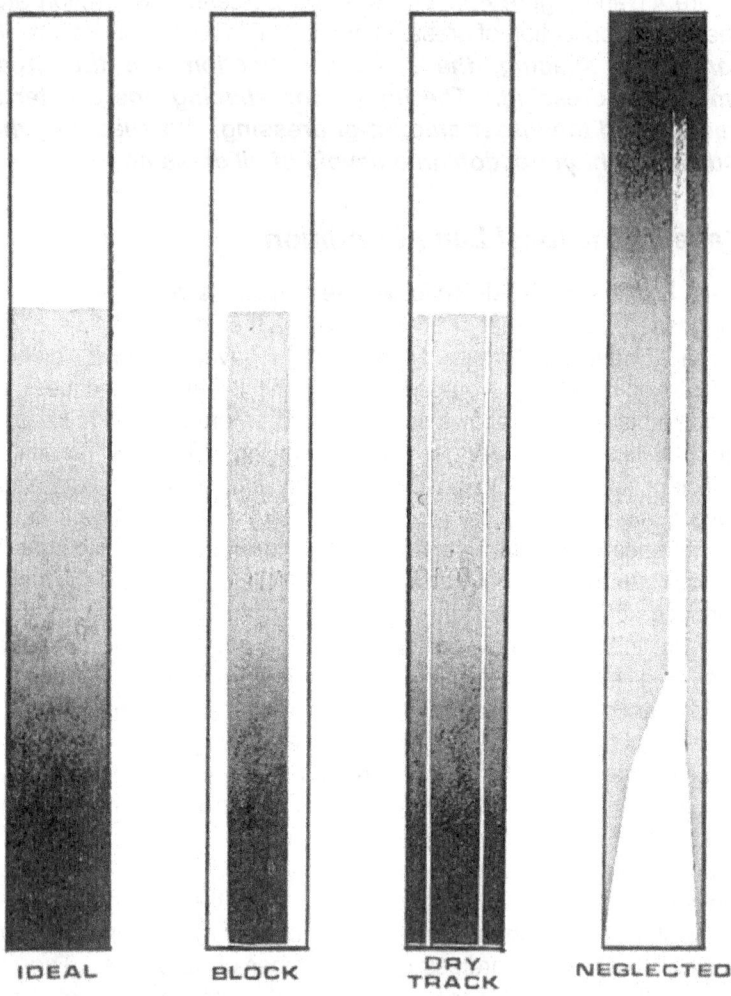

IDEAL   BLOCK   DRY TRACK   NEGLECTED

I feel that the harder plastic finishes are not used with the bowler in mind. Rather, the finishes are used so that less maintenance is necessary. Harder, more durable, lane finishes require fewer resurfacings within a given period of time, and this is an advantage. However, oil will neither penetrate this type of finish nor produce the desired condition with cross-buffing. (It is no wonder that some proprietors have resorted to blocking this type of lane finish. No honest, consistent lane condition is possible when the oil travels toward the pins with such rapidity!) The buffed lacquer lane condition gave no one an advantage. Full rollers as well as semirollers had an equal chance at good scoring. Anyone who could get his own skills together could score better and better with practice because a good delivery usually produced good results (this is not necessarily the case with a blocked lane). Speed of the ball was not as critical, and a crisper delivery was possible. I realize that lacquer is rapidly becoming a thing of the past, but plastics research now has the capability to produce a lane finish that will hold oil even longer than lacquer did. If technology can produce this softer or more porous type of material, we may see the return of a lane condition on which any type of effective delivery can score well, and on which the softer-surfaced balls are not necessary. In passing, let me emphasize an important point — no matter what material is used for lane maintenance and conditioning, only hard-working, intelligent proprietors will provide the bowler the best possible and fair lane conditions. The lazy, uninterested proprietors are the ones who take shortcuts (neglect or blocking), and the bowler suffers for it. Since you will never bowl on the ideal lane condition, and since near-ideal lanes pose minimal adaptation problems, I will make only brief comments concerning adaptive variables. Moderate hardness (75 – 85) rubber or plastic balls are equally effective whether or not a full rolling or semirolling ball is used. Likewise, there should be a playing angle for most bowlers so that hitting the pocket and carrying the pins seems to be an easily attainable goal. Any further comment concerning the ideal lane condition would just be a complete lesson on how you should bowl; that is not what this chapter is about, so let's move on to a consideration of the blocked lane.

Case 2: The Blocked Lane Condition

This is sometimes called a walled condition or a put-up shot. It is a condition in which the ball, in its procession down the lane, is influenced to hit the pocket by the pattern of applied dressing. The degree of this condition ranges from a moderate taper (or feather or blend) to a blatant application of the oil through a stencil or by a cut applicator. I am opposed to this condition, not because of its value in promoting high scores, but because of its effects on the performance of different classes of bowlers. On blocked lanes, for example, a fair bowler who rolls a large hook usually stands a better chance against a good bowler who rolls a small hook. This is especially true in tournaments where handicap is added to the fair bowler's score. I have seen this happen innumerable times, and the result is always the same — everybody loses! As an example, I bowled an entire league season on blocked lanes, averaging 206 (I didn't know how to use them). Another fellow in the same league whose previous high book average had been 168, averaged 212. Besides, he was using a fourteen-pound semispinner ball as opposed to my sixteen-pound high semiroller. Did he practice more? No, rather he felt that he had improved so much that he did not need to practice as much! When the city tournament was held in another establishment, he failed to bowl 500 for any of his three-game series. Further, when the blocks were eliminated the next bowling season, he quit bowling entirely! I averaged 208 without the benefit of the blocks. (I guess I was wiser by then.) Another example is a big, powerful young bowler who carried a 210 average on the blocked lanes and a 185-or-less average in each of four other leagues held in four different establishments. I could continue recounting examples of how bowling exclusively on blocked conditions gives a bowler an incorrect impression of his ability. This can have a disastrous effect on the young, aspiring bowler because his mind does not mature along with his scoring ability. Practicing on a blocked lane does have its value in working out problems in alignment, the swing, and timing; and the capability of scoring high occasionally is something everyone should experience, but there is something wrong with the bowler who needs a blocked lane to bowl well. **The dry track is another type of blocked condition.** It is one that takes a little more skill to obtain the advantage, and this is discussed further below. The diagrams show the differences between the blocked and the dry track conditions. I feel like the Devil's advocate in telling you how to play a blocked lane. Actually, it is not difficult to figure out the best playing angle just from looking at the second diagram of Figure 41 The main objective is to obtain the largest margin of error, that is, if one rolls the ball to the right of the target he desires that the ball hook more to reach the pocket. Likewise, if he misses his target to the left, he wants the ball to hook less or slide (skid) more so that the pocket will still be hit squarely. This indicates to you that the best target lies directly on the edge of the oil and that the line should be roughly parallel with the edge. The only time when this parallel relationship is not maintained is to make minor adjustments for carrying or for breaking down of the condition. Naturally, the target line changes, depending on where the edge of the oil block is. The term, "blocked five-to-five" means that the oil is applied in the middle of the lane and between the two outermost arrows (the fifth boards). A "zero-to-five block" would give a distinct advantage to right-handed bowlers since their margin for error would be better than that for left-handed bowlers. The reverse is true for a "five-to-zero block."

Telltale Signs: Any totally inside target line is completely useless because the ball will only skid in the inside area. A cross-lane shot to a corner spare must be direct or the ball may miss the pin or pins. Any outside shot hooks more than the inside shot, but the ball delivered toward center spares will hook more than that to left or right-of-center spares because of the usual cross-lane move to align for the spares. In other words, the lane hooks more from the outside than from the inside if the lane is blocked to favor the outside shot. The ball generally hooks more the farther outside the target line is moved. This is not the case with the dry track, or tunnel block. Like the block, the best target lies on the edge of the block, but the outsides also have oil applied so that it is possible to roll a ball too far to the outside. It takes a better bowler to take advantage of this type of block, but it is still a form of help. The third diagram of Figure 41 shows a dry track block that is designed to favor both right and left-handed bowlers, but any type of modification is possible to favor one or the other.

Tendency: When bowling too frequently on a blocked lane the tendency is to put more and more finesse on the swing and release as the bowler places the ball on the edge of the oil. This must be avoided If one is to preserve his adaptability for other, more demanding conditions. Try not to weaken your delivery.

Possible Alternatives: Target Line – discussed above, also there is a successful line on the blocked lane no matter how large the hook. Adjusting is a matter of trying different outside targets and lines until the proper one is found. Delivery Variables – Speed is determined by the carrying percentage rather than by the necessity to adjust the amount of hook. I suggest moderate speed combined with moderate V and a little turn at the release. This combination delays the hook slightly so that a little more momentum is given to the ball at impact. I have suggested moderate positions (that you should probably try to use on most lane conditions anyway) so that you can make adjustments as necessary to preserve carrying power. Blocked lanes have a marked tendency to become difficult to carry strikes on; this is due to a movement of oil near the pins (due to consistently hitting the same area of the lane at that level), and it is also probably caused by an unreliable subconscious action of the bowler to use finesse or soften his shot. In the first case, adjustment of the target line is necessary; and, in the latter, adjustment of the delivery variables is best. With the dry track, the best target line is directly in the center of the dry board area and parallel with the boards; an inside-to-outside shot is not successful in achieving a consistent pocket-hitting percentage, and an outside-to-inside shot toward the pocket simply fights the tendency of the lane to direct the ball. Since it takes a more straightaway line to utilize this dry track (and, consequently, a better bowler), a little more lift and turn may be necessary to make the ball hit with more impact. This is because there is less dry area to allow the ball to hook on its own. Greater V and turn, combined with moderate or less speed gives the bowler a slight edge.

Ball Characteristics: Both rubber and plastic balls can be used effectively on any blocked condition with the plastic ball probably carrying the pins a little more effectively. The hardness, porosity, and composition of the shell needed depends on the traction of the dry areas of the lane finish. A harder ball is appropriate for a softer finish, and a softer-shelled ball is more appropriate for a harder finish. The objective in choosing a particular hardness is to accentuate the difference in the hooking action between the dry and oily areas of the blocked lane. **This is generally the reason that softer balls were developed in the first place — to maximize the difference between high and low traction areas.** Let me say at this point that I believe bowlers are using too soft-shelled balls. When a bowler saw his hook literally straighten out on the harder (and much oiler) lane finishes, his natural reaction was to switch to the easily available soft ball. Unfortunately, the pendulum swung too far, and great numbers of bowlers used balls too soft for many conditions not suited for it. The bowler's speed, lift, and turn adjusted to the demands of the soft ball, and his adaptability has suffered. I predict that, as lane finishes are researched further, more durable yet softer finishes (or more porous — something that holds the oil dressing) will be developed; and the bowler will have to change to a more moderate hardness ball, and his delivery will again change in response.

Case 3: The Neglected Lane Condition

This can be just about any type of lane condition that results from ignorance of lane maintenance procedures or just from sloppy habits. The most unfortunate aspect is that these practices are so diverse and widespread that I cannot generalize about them effectively; the diagram of Figure 41 is probably not a very accurate representation, either. One definite statement can be made — these conditions give the bowler the least value for his money. Since this condition does not allow the ball to act as it should, the serious bowler finds that conditioning his delivery is almost impossible. To learn a skill, one must be able to predict what will happen if he experiments with small changes in certain variables connected with that skill. If these small changes in a bowler's delivery do not produce consistent results (and neglected lane conditions never do), improvement and development of confidence to a high degree is unattainable.

Because the scoring potential is always low, the high average bowler is at a distinct disadvantage on a neglected condition. He finds that he is competing on a par with lower average bowlers whose scoring potential more closely matches the maximum scoring potential of the lanes they are bowling on. Good bowlers, as Lou Bellisimo said, "begin to bowl like clowns!" Usually, they find it difficult to average above the middle 180s, so it is easy to see how much of an equalizer neglected conditions are — 180 and 200-average bowlers fighting it out in the same ring, so to speak.

You know, it has always angered me when a 150-average manager of one of these "boneyard" establishments tells me that I should be able to adjust to the conditions. Adjust to what? The lanes are not consistent from one to another; the conditions on none of them let the ball act as it should — hook later, hit the pocket, and carry pins consistently, and, besides, the approaches are usually slippery with built-up dust and grit. "Being able to adjust..."and "If you can bowl here, you can bowl anywhere..." are simply cliches to this manager who may never realize their meanings. To adjust, one must attain a certain level of excellence, which, by his average, this man has not reached. Better bowlers eventually leave these dens of depression because there is nothing to hold their interest. I advise any serious aspiring bowler to leave also. Do not join leagues if it involves more than an occasional substitution. If you do, it will only cause you to place emphasis on the social aspect, and this discourages the discipline necessary for the development of concentration and a

149

positive self-image. In these ill-managed establishments, when lanes are newly resurfaced or recoated, the first few applications of oil are the only ones acceptable because sufficient neglectful buildup has not had time to form. Until that time, scoring is not as difficult because the lanes are more consistent. With time, application of new oil over old, and lack of desire of the management to provide this most important service to the bowler (consistently good conditions), the lanes settle down into their old pattern, and scoring becomes difficult again. I feel strongly that to protect the interests of the bowler, to promote the spirit of competitiveness, and to improve the image of the sport, the American Bowling Congress should rescind the sanction of any establishment that allows their lanes to be so low-scoring. Just as the block is prohibited because of its harm to the image of the sport and because of its tendency to make scores meaningless, the neglected or "reverse block" should be prohibited also. If the aim of the ABC is to bring more bowlers into the sport, it must further protect their interests. The neglected condition actually does more damage to the bowler in terms of ingraining undesirable habits than does the blocked condition, and the bowler must also be protected against this type of condition, as well as the proprietors who perpetuate it — they have not done anything for the sport and probably never will (except for padding their own pockets)! Proper lane conditioning is an investment — not an expense.

Telltale Signs: Low carrying percentage on pocket hits from any angle because of oil buildup on the pindecks. Such low traction pindecks keep the pins from toppling before leaving the pindeck, and this lessens the chance of the pins hitting each other. The ball tends to hook early because of the lack of oil on the heads. The area of the head where the ball contacts the lane may be worn and blackened due to the lack of oil. Delivery on a target line through the track area (between the ninth and fourteenth boards) results in an early hook, while the oil buildup farther down the lane either keeps the ball from hitting the pocket squarely or it keeps the ball from hooking across the headpin when the target is missed on the inside. Outside the track, the ball hooks less because the oil buildup on the outside boards is almost the entire length of the lane. Washouts are more frequent as are the 2-pin combinations. Rolling the ball on an inside line shows even earlier hooking, and the shallower angle to the pocket in conjunction with the oil buildup on the pindeck allows too much deflection for the ball to effectively carry the pins. Splits, which are more frequent anyway, become even more so with the inside line.

Tendency: In playing this condition, there is a strong tendency of the bowler to point the ball toward the pocket from the outside or extreme outside line; and there is just as strong a tendency for him to roll the ball with too much speed and lessen the lift in the improper way (called "dumping") when using an inside line. This dumping of the ball probably results from a faster downswing being mismatched to the footwork; therefore, the ball reaches the foul line too soon — sooner than the sliding foot. Since this is one of the non-variable characteristics (timing), the bowler should not let this happen just for the purpose of playing a neglected lane. Another tendency is to change the angle of the swing to one that crosses the body (if using the outside line) or to one that is behind the back and that forces the follow through to the outside (when using an inside line). ***The swing should ideally never be affected by adaptation to a lane condition, but it can be if the lane condition is bowled on too frequently.***

Possible Alternatives: Target Lines and Delivery Variables – When employing any inside line, I suggest that you try to delay the hook as late as possible to strengthen carrying power. The best way to do this, I have found, is to minimize V and use a greater amount of turn; more speed can be used if necessary. Since the inside line is most dependable on this type of condition, I recommend this line as the first alternative. If the pin decks are extremely oily and if splits are really a problem, try to hit the headpln lightly — do not try to attack the pocket squarely; the hits will not carry if direct, and the chance of hooking onto the headpin is too great. Take your chances with mixing pins, avoiding splits, and leaving one or two-pin spares that you can convert. If you are using the outside lines, try to stay out of the track until the ball has traveled quite a way down the lane. It is probably best to use a fifth-board target (or even further outside) and roll the ball toward a light pocket hit. When using either inside or outside lines, one should remember to stay out of the track area until as late as possible; this area is very inconsistent, and is probably the best angle for leaving splits and washouts.

Ball Characteristics: For use with any target line, I recommend that you use one of moderate to slightly harder surface properties. For the inside line, I have had some success with a hard rubber ball (87 durometer reading and above). It seems to help in delaying the hook; and pins fly off of it with higher velocity, increasing the chances for a mixing strike. I would suggest a plastic ball of similar hardness for use with the outside line that is pointed toward the light pocket. The plastic ball skids farther but reacts more strongly when it hits the track area close to the pocket. Definitely, however, avoid the use of a soft rubber ball from the inside angle, and also avoid using a soft plastic ball in the track or farther outside lest it overreact and leave more splits.

Final Comment: I must apologize for not giving you more effective instructions. None of the shots I have discussed are really good, but they will minimize problems. They keep you from wasting time with other less effective angles — they keep you from scoring too badly under the circumstances. No other condition taxes the bowler's patience any more than the neglected condition, and it will be a real challenge to you to keep concentrating. Keep your composure, try to concentrate, and it will pay off with good scores relative to the low scoring potential of the lane. Play the percentages and keep the ball light in the pocket; do not try to fit the ball squarely into the pocket — you'll be sorry!

Case 4: The Oil-Soaked Lane Condition

This is a condition that we do not see as often today as in days past. Then, lanes were resurfaced with lacquer and kept saturated with oil for two or three weeks to prevent tracking while the lacquer cured. Today, the epoxy or urethane finishes cure in a few hours, so there is no need to keep the lanes so saturated. Early morning shifts at tournaments may still have the oily condition because the proprietors may be trying to get through the day's shifts without adding oil. How ridiculous! The tournament managers shouldn't schedule so many shifts

Telltale Signs: There is really not much to say about this condition. In a nutshell, the ball skids too far, hooks too little, and carries poorly, partly because of the lack of sufficient revolutions. The pins tend to slide off the deck rather than topple, so pinfall is lessened with any type of hit. Placement of the ball on the lane is important because a small deviation from the target can mean the ball will completely miss the headpin; in other words, there is little margin for error.

Tendency: The bowler must consciously avoid the tendency to force the lift, and therefore pull the shot, because this type of condition favors over-exaggeration.

Possible Alternatives: Target Line – I recommend the extreme outside target with the line pointed slightly toward the pocket to maximize the angle of attack. Delivery Variables – I suggest the use of maximum V, a good amount of roll, and moderate to less speed. This helps to make the angle of attack steeper, and, even then, the angle will not be as steep as a comfortably-delivered ball on an ideal lane condition. The use of maximum side roll (lift and turn) is difficult to control, so you must learn to live with inconsistency (and a certain amount of tension in the swing) when bowling on the extremely oily condition.

Figure 42: Three Additional Lane Conditions – The last diagram shows a sequence of playing angles.

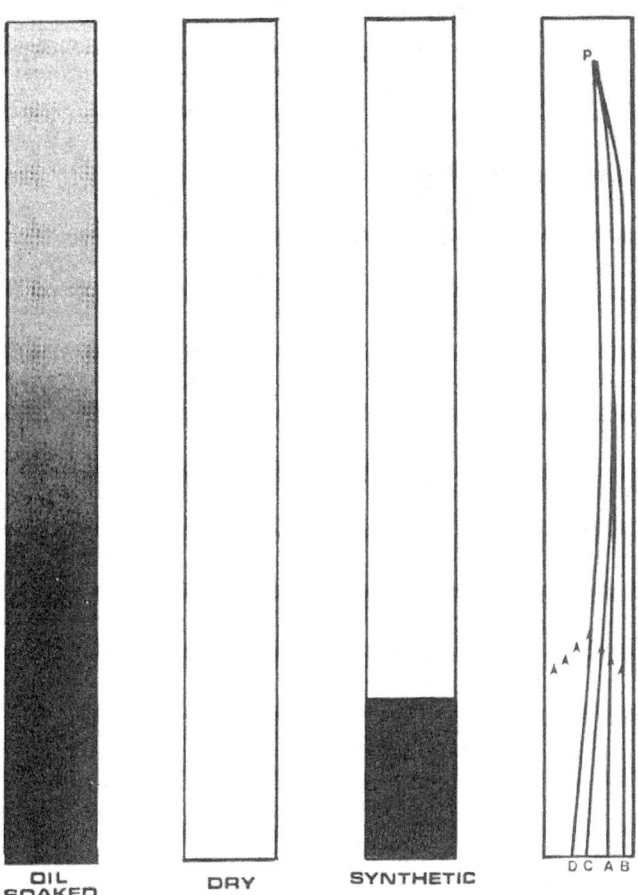

Ball Characteristics: Use the softest or most porous plastic or rubber ball allowable. Avoid the use of a hard rubber ball on oily conditions; the hard plastic ball may hook more strongly and carry a greater percentage of strikes.

Case 5: The Dry Lane Condition

This is the condition that hooks so much. It is common in Europe where the better bowlers have used conventional grips to cut down on the amount of lift.

Telltale Signs: First, the ball hooks so early that it may deviate from the target line before it rolls over the target point. The more traction on the head area, the more the tendency for lift to deviate the ball from the line. I have seen a ball take a quick jump to the left at the initial contact with the lane when a strong right-handed bowler delivered it onto a dry lane. Secondly, the ball attacks the pocket at such a steep angle from the outside that corner pins are left with great frequency on pocket hits. With the inside angle, early hook and rollout of the ball makes it less effective on impact; and pocket splits such as the 4-9 and 4-7-10 are more common due to the lack of deflection.

Tendency: The bowler tends to either use more speed than he is capable of, or he lofts the ball out on the lane by changing the timing of the swing (if you remember, this may cause a swinging of the shoulders because the ball is too far behind the sliding foot at the foul line).

Possible Alternatives: Target Lines and Delivery Characteristics – The bowler can employ minimum V, hold a 12:00 o'clock thumb position, use more forward speed, and use a second arrow target line. This gives a straighter rolling ball with minimum hook. Or, he can move the target line to an extreme outside position, use moderate V, and turn the ball slightly to delay the hook. The speed should be maintained a little faster, if possible. A third alternative is to move the target line to an inside or extreme inside position, minimize V, and maximize the turn to delay the hook as late as possible. In this case, the speed should be faster than normal. In any of these target line/hand position/speed combinations, the objective is to hit the pocket, but carrying will be a problem. With the inside and extreme outside angles, tight pocket leaves and corner pins, respectively, will be a constant source of irritation. With the second arrow line, the lane must favor an early-rolling short hook that attacks the pocket at a shallow angle, or carrying will also be a source of irritation.

Ball Characteristics: The harder the shell, the better. Less hook is desired, but preferably without taking any of the roll off of the shot. This is best accomplished with a harder ball. I prefer a hard rubber ball, but you may prefer plastic on this type of condition.

Case 6: The Synthetic Lane

At this writing, many companies have initiated promotional programs designed to sell their new synthetic lanes. These are made of material closely related to the Formica used on counter tops; they are non-porous and extremely hard. The manufacturers claim that bowlers enjoy the game more on these lanes because of more consistent scoring, less dirt, less oil dressing, etc. All of these factors are fine, but I have found (at least on the early version of the synthetic lane) that the approaches are normally a bit on the slippery side, and they can be very sticky, depending on what is used to clean them. The pin decks are slick, regardless of the absence of oil, and the pins do not topple quickly enough to take many other pins along with them into the pit. **Most important, however, is the fact that these lanes do not hook enough, no matter what hardness of legal ball is used on them, unless the lift is exaggerated.** In all fairness, I must concede that the above may be simple technical problems that can be eliminated with further research and testing. These lanes may promote better average scoring while narrowing the gap between high and low scores. I believe there will be occasional high scores, but with a lesser frequency than almost any other consistent condition, and this is probably going to be due to their holding (less hooking) tendency. Sadly, even if all problems are solved, will the synthetic-lane bowler be as good a bowler as the one who has had to adapt to various types of conditions? What will his adaptive range be when he can play all (synthetic) lanes with exactly the same shot?

(***Author's Note:*** In the last 30 years, many changes have been made in the synthetic materials comprising lane surfaces. While still very slick when oiled and tricky as oil is being carried down, synthetic lanes are the norm, with high scores being the result of contemporary oiling patterns in response to the use of reactive resin balls.)

Tendency: There is a marked tendency to force the follow through because the lane does not hook sharply at the end near the pins with the comfortable delivery. A forced follow-through (the pulled shot) hooks early, however, and causes the ball to finish high on the headpin.

Possible Alternatives: Target Lines and Delivery Characteristics – One can play just about any angle he chooses, but the outside lines seem to carry more effectively. Moderation is the key because of the tendency to make the ball hook with a forced follow-through. I suggest the use of moderate V, a slight amount of turn to delay the hook and increase the attack angle, and moderate to slow speed.

Ball Characteristics: A plastic ball can overreact more easily on the synthetic lane, so if you use one, try to use one that is on the harder side. I favor the use of a soft rubber ball with a little more finger weight and side weight.

Becoming Perceptive

One becomes perceptive in bowling in the same way that he learns any process that is new to him. The following have, in fact, been adapted from what professional educators call the "Process Skills", so don't give me all of the credit for innovating them!

1. **Observe:** Watch others to see what the results are when they deliver the ball. Golfers call this "going to school on a shot." Learn to watch how one variable relates to another. Match one variable with another; the combinations are almost endless. Learn to identify what variables are controlled and which cannot be controlled. Watching bowlers can take on a new meaning!

2. **Measure the relationships:** Learn to what extent changing one variable influences another. Although accurate measurements may not be possible in most cases, useful estimates can be made

3. **Classify what you observe:** Learn to make your own generalizations about what you see and do. In doing so, talk it over with someone. Do not make a generalization from improper logic, i.e. do not infer that changing one variable necessarily influences the other. This is the way reverse logic is developed, and this can impede progress. Be sure of what you see!

4. *Learn to communicate what you generalize:* Discussing a problem is the best way to begin to solve it, but you must know how to describe it in understandable terms. This is the reason that I hate slang terms in bowling — they have different meanings to different persons. (I am sorry that I have had to use some in this book).

5. *Predict what you can do based on what you have generalized from your observations:* Can you do what the other fellow can do? Make your own predictions in this manner, "If, I turn my hand under the ball, will it reduce the amount of hook?" This is the questioning of the cause/effect relationship.

6. *Control the variables as much as possible:* This means that you should vary only one thing at a time so your observations can be as clear as possible. Only by controlling all of the other variables (footwork, timing, V, etc.) can you begin to measure the results of varying the one under consideration. This is the reason why you should return to a familiar lane to work out problems in your delivery.

7. *Experiment:* This is self-explanatory. Never be afraid to bowl under different conditions or to change various aspects of your delivery or equipment. This is the essence of development! If necessary, write down observations of your own experimentation — don't forget each evening what you learned that day.

8. *Interpret the results of your experimentation:* This is the sorting out process that involves all of the previous steps. This is also what I have been talking about when I urge you to know your own capabilities. In time, all of these steps will be automatic (as they already are with the best bowlers whether they admit it or not). Commit them to memory and use them as best you can.

9. *"Keep it instinctive":* This is advice from my good friend, former team captain, PBA champion, Texas match game champion, and high average leader in the NBL, J. B. Solomon. He meant that, once you have learned the fundamentals and learned yourself, do not treat the sport as an exact science. If you do, you are missing the enjoyment, and are apt to think yourself out of becoming as good as you should. When I asked former ABC all-events champion and

Hall of Famer, Tony Lindemann about making corrections to the shot according to exacting requirements such as adjusting the target one-quarter of a board, he said not to do it, "you get bugs!"

(*Author's Note:* Reflecting on Solomon's and Lindemann's statements, I now believe that they were not criticizing an analytical approach to the game; they were simply advising not to think about too much while competing — especially during the delivery. In the 30 years since **Perceptive Bowling** hit the market, I have learned how to reduce the number of cues to attend to, and I teach my students how to do the same.)

The Serious Commitment – Give Yourself Every Opportunity

If you are really serious about being a well-rounded, proficient bowler, I wish you would take some time to consider the following bits of philosophy. They may or may not wind up being incorporated into your own, but they can give you a point of departure. I mention some sources of information that have helped me greatly and that I hope continue to help me as the years pass. I invite you to try these suggestions because you will never know how good you can be unless you give yourself every opportunity to do your best.

1. **Set realistic goals for yourself:** If you are bowling scores that are close to, but not quite, what you expect, ask yourself why. Remember that scoring is relative only to the scoring potential of the lanes you are bowling on. Also, don't expect to beat whom you feel is not as good a bowler but who practices more than yourself or whose style is better adapted to a particular condition. It is ridiculous to declare one bowler better than another simply on the basis of a small difference in average. This can become an erroneous self-evaluation that is not even a part of self-improvement.

2. **Try to eliminate problems that interfere with your concentration:** If you have family or financial problems, it may be difficult to turn your entire thought process to the bowling game. It is easy for someone to tell you to concentrate, but to do it when faced with problems can be impossible for even the best bowler.

3. *Get the proper amount of sleep:* Only with a well-rested mind and body can you begin to condition yourself to concentrate. The first thing that goes haywire from lack of sleep is the timing. You may get by with loss of a little sleep for one night, but you cannot neglect to get the proper amount for extended periods of time. You can't beat it, so don't try it!

4. *Get the proper nutrition:* Only with proper vitamins, minerals, and protein can you maximize your abilities to perform in stress situations. Additionally, I can almost guarantee that proper nutrition combined with proper sleep will help you concentrate noticeably better. If you don't believe me, ask Carmen Salvino. Better yet, read any book by Dr. Roger J. Williams, former head of the biochemistry department at the University of Texas at Austin. One of his works I highly recommend is *Nutrition Against Disease.* If you cannot find it, read his *The Wonderful World Within You.*

5. *Condition yourself properly to concentrate:* Are you surprised that you have to learn to concentrate? You cannot make yourself concentrate no matter what bowling books and instructors say! Jack Heise's *How You Can Bowl Better Using Self-Hypnosis* is an absolute must for any bowler who expects to improve. He shows you how to concentrate, how to change aspects of your delivery, how to improve your self-image, etc.

(*Author's Note:* Apply the principles outlined in *Bowling Tough: Three Simple Methods to Improve Your Performance Under Pressure* by *Will Powers and Bob Strickland*)

Other methods that are very useful are those presented in books by Maxwell Maltz and in books on the techniques of yoga breathing. You do not have to be a yoga practitioner to enjoy the benefits of yoga breathing; musicians, pilots, baseball players, etc. use it, and you can too!

6. *Give yourself every opportunity to develop your adaptive range:* When you have learned how to condition a well-rested and well-nourished mind to concentrate via self-hypnosis, you are ready to learn how to adapt to different lane conditions. Bowl on as many different types of condition as possible, and in as many different contexts as possible — team play, doubles play, singles tournaments, pot games, challenge matches. You

cannot have an adaptive range unless you go out and develop it!

7. ***Don't get discouraged:*** All too often, one gets the impression that bad habits that creep into a person's game are unique to him. Actually, everyone experiences the same problems with the bowling delivery, equipment, etc. In fact, assignment of the word "bad" to incorrectness of form is unfortunate because it tends to give more importance to the flaw than it deserves. Remember that repetition of the correct actions minimize the flaws in your game, so try to retain a good instructor.

10 Instructions in Measuring and Drilling

I sincerely hope that you are satisfied with your present grip, whether it be standard, Collier, Sarge Easter, or something else. However, after having read the previous chapters, you may be interested in trying my version of the offset thumbhole grip.

(**Author's Note:** In the years following the publication of **Perceptive Bowling** in 1980, many critics voiced their opinions about my offset thumbhole grip, calling it a "delusion", an "imaginary grip", and a "simple function of the difference in spans", among other rationalizations. They made the grip "controversial" when there is absolutely nothing to argue about! *The grip exists, and that is the end of the story. Read the rest of this chapter, and you may agree!*

Most criticisms came from people "in the business" that never took time to read carefully and understand that *the difference is in the necessary pitch relationships* to make the hand comfortable and most effective in terms of leverage. They simply had hardened opinions that they were most eager to conserve. The grip was endorsed by many others in the United States and Europe, even though some did not drill it correctly. I thank these insightful folks for their confidence and for defending my opinions over the years.)

If you drill your own grips and are therefore, a hobbyist, just reading the following instructions may be of some interest. The steps, designed to be followed in "cookbook" fashion, are different from any other drilling instructions I have ever seen. Explanations and drawings are included that try to illustrate the reasoning behind each operation. If you do not drill your own grips but still desire to try this one, take these instructions to your favorite driller. He should be

161

capable of working with you to give you what you want. If he does not want to take the time, or if he shows no interest in learning how to drill a new grip, find yourself another driller with a more open mind. I admit that some of the procedures that I have outlined may seem tedious to the experienced driller, but I have chosen to present them in a detailed fashion so they are clear to the novice. Additionally, the steps are more adaptable for use with different drilling machines, since they are based on realigning the ball in the holding cradle before drilling each hole. This realignment also emphasizes the necessity for each hole to have its own plane of pitch.

(**Author's Note:** Stop! You may ask at this point, *"Can't I drill this "offset thumbhole" relationship, using the standard grip layout centerline?"* Surely, you can; just select the correct pitches! First, however, you need to drill a ball, following the directions, below, so you can find out what those pitches are! Remember, it requires more than just rotating the planes of fingerhole pitch away and to the inside of the thumb; you must move the forward/reverse pitch plane of the thumbhole away from the bridge, more toward the center of the middle fingerhole, as well. Then, the grip is truly an offset thumbhole grip!)

To Drill a Strickland Offset Thumbhole Grip, Follow These Steps in the Order Presented

1. *Select the ball based on desired hardness, surface texture, cover material, total weight, top weight, and type of core.*

2. *Measure the hardness and record this on the grip layout measurement sheet.* Take several readings and use the average. Calibrate the durometer before testing the ball.

3. *Weigh the ball to ensure the correct position of the punch mark and record the measured amount of top weight on the sheet.* If the punch mark is incorrectly placed, indicate the proper position with a wax pencil mark (a "C"). This mark indicates the true beginning weight center position.

4. *Measure spans, select hole sizes and pitches, and record these on the sheet.* Use Table 5 at the back of this chapter if you desire. Calculate the amount of weight removed by the holes and record these figures on the sheet for use with step 6. It is advisable to exercise the hand with a spring or molded rubber exerciser prior to measuring for span. The state of

tension of the hand can mean as much as 1/4" difference in span.

(*Author's Note:* For modern-day bowling balls, you may skip steps 5, 6, and 7 if you are following weight distribution layout instructions provided by a manufacturer. In this case, simply mark the midpoint of the grip layout centerline "G3" and proceed to step 8)

5. ***Using a Bill Taylor Weight Label Shifter or a similar device, calculate the necessary amount of shift of the grip center off of the weight center to obtain the desired finger/thumb and lateral weight imbalance.*** Indicate the grip center with a wax penciled "G1." Remember that the grip center of the right-handed offset thumbhole grip is slightly left of a standard grip center.

6. ***Correct the position of the grip center for weight center shift resulting from the hole size weight shift.*** Use Table 5. See "Incidental Weight Shift" in chapter seven, Figure 30, and Figure 31. The weight center moves in the direction of the lesser removal of weight. Use Taylor's Weight Label Shifter or a similar device to reposition the grip center. Mark the new one "G2" with a wax pencil, and erase the "G1."

7. ***Correct the position of the grip center for weight center shift resulting from the influence of pitches.*** Use Table 6 at the back of this chapter. The weight center moves in the direction of pitch. The repositioned grip center should be marked "G3" with a wax pencil and the "G2" erased. See Figure 43, A. If there is extreme reverse pitch in the thumbhole and extreme forward pitch in the finger-holes, this shift can be significant. See the discussion of this factor under "Incidental Weight Shift" in chapter seven.

8. ***Draw the grip layout centerline (CL) slightly to the right of "G3" so as to superimpose the offset thumbhole grip center on the "G3" mark itself.*** The leading edge of the thumbhole and the center of a line tangent to the leading edges of the fingerholes should be equidistant from the "G3." See Figure 43, B

Figure 43: A. The grip layout centerline (CL) is drawn slightly to the right of the offset thumbhole grip center (G3). For a right-handed grip, G3 should be located as shown if finger weight and side weight are desired. (L = the label) B. Span Lines (SL) and bridge lines (BL) are added. C. The thumbhole pitch plane reference line (MT) is drawn. D. The ring fingerhole span line lies on an arc (R) drawn with the near edge of the thumbhole as the pivot point.

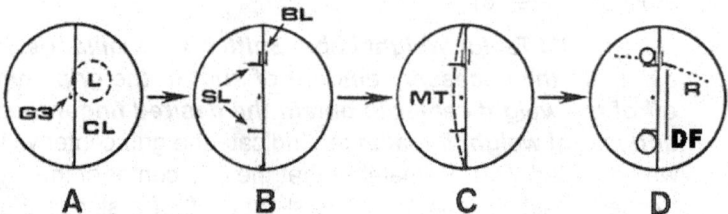

9. **Draw span lines perpendicular to the grip centerline to mark the leading edges of the thumbhole and middle fingerhole.** Draw bridge lines parallel with the centerline. See Figure 43, B.

10. **Draw another line (MT) that bisects the centers of the thumbhole and middle fingerhole; make allowance for the bridge.** This line marks the plane of reference for the thumbhole pitches. It is to be used only for aligning the ball for the drilling of the thumbhole and is not used for any other purpose. See Figure 43, C.

11. **Drill the thumbhole using line MT as the centerline alignment guide in the ball cradle.** Thumbhole pitches measure true because line MT is a fully circumferential line (actually an arc), the plane of which would pass through the geometric center of the ball as does plane CL. See diagrams D and E, Figure 15.

12. **Remeasure the span to the middle fingerhole to correct for small errors in drilling the thumbhole.** Set the lateral pitch on zero and select the desired forward/reverse pitch for the middle fingerhole. Align the ball in the holding cradle using the true centerline (CL) as the centerline alignment guide. The drill tip should be directly over the center of the bridge. The lateral pitch adjustment should be turned so that the hole will be centered tangent to the bridge and span lines. The middle fingerhole plane will be parallel with the centerline plane (CL) and will not lie on a circumferential plane. See Figure 15,

chapter four. Forward/reverse pitch of the middle fingerhole measures true, and the lateral pitch will measure one-half of the bridge plus one-half the diameter of the hole.

13. **Drill the middle fingerhole.** Break the surface of the ball slowly with the drill tip to ensure that the hole edges are tangent to the span and bridge lines. Note the relationships shown in Figure 15. To summarize:

    a. The middle fingerhole and thumbhole are aligned on the surface of the ball by the line MT.

    b. The thumbhole pitch is related to plane MT and the geometric center of the ball, but not to plane CL.

    c. The middle fingerhole is parallel with plane CL but bears no further relationship to plane MT.

14. **Draw a span line (R) for the ring fingerhole.** Use a hooked span scale and a wax pencil as a sort of compass. The edge of the thumbhole should be the pivot point, and the span line will lie on an arc. See Figure 43, D.

15. **Determine the direction of flex of the ring finger, and draw a line from the leading edge of the ring fingerhole span line in this direction.** This determination may take a little time. The direction may change as the hand is closed, so it should be measured as the hand is simulating the grip as closely as possible. If the determination is correct, the forward/reverse pitch of this hole will be exactly parallel with the direction of flex, and the hole will be comfortable without excess pressure on either side of the finger.

    (**Author's Note:** The forward/reverse plane of the ring fingerhole of a normal hand is usually parallel with that of the middle fingerhole. However, it is not inappropriate to point the ring fingerhole slightly toward the thumb.)

16. **Set the lateral pitch adjustment of the machine to zero, and select the desired forward/reverse pitch.** Set the ball in the holding cradle using Line DF (for "direction of flex") as the centerline alignment guide.

17. **Drill the ring fingerhole.** Break the surface of the ball slowly with the drill tip to ensure that the hole edges are tangent to the bridge line and span line (or arc). If the fingerholes are drilled 1-1/2 inches deep (as is standard in a fingertip grip), they

should not run together at the bottom, even if the direction of flex of the ring finger is toward the thumb. Deeper holes such as the 2- 3 inch-deep conventional fingerholes may run together, so they should probably be drilled parallel with each other.

18. *Take the ball out of the drilling machine,* return all settings to a central position (usually zero), return all drills to the proper places, and clean up the area.

A Word On Pitch

Why did I not list specific combinations of forward/reverse and lateral pitches in the form of actual settings? As I said in chapter four, it would be ridiculous for me to recommend specific pitches when there is no effective way to determine it. Likewise, exact settings can lose their meaning when discussing more than one type of drilling machine. Forward/reverse fingerhole pitch is determined by the feel of the lifting fingers in correctly-fitted spans. Lateral pitch of the middle fingerhole should be determined by its parallelism to the centerline plane. Lateral pitch of the ring fingerhole should be determined by its direction of flex. If the procedures that I listed are followed, any drilling machine can be used; the ball is rotated to a new plane of pitch for each hole, thus fitting the requirements of the hand. If one desires to know what his pitches are in terms of numbers and the standard two planes of pitch, he simply has to measure them and record the figures on the grip measurement sheet.

A Comparison of the Standard Grip, the Strickland Offset Thumbhole Grip, and the Brunswick Offset Thumbhole Grip

Figure 44 presents three versions of the same grip with respect to spans and hole sizes. For the sake of illustration, let's assume that the pitches of all of the thumbholes are zero. In each of the three grips, the pitch of the thumbhole measures true zero because the planes upon which they lie pass through the geometric center of the ball. Could they possibly feel the same, however? No, because of the different positioning of the top of the thumbholes in relation to the positions and pitches of the fingerholes! The standard thumbhole is superimposed on the grip layout centerline; my offset thumbhole is tangent to this line; and the Brunswick offset thumbhole is located an arbitrary one-quarter inch from the line.

Figure 44: A Comparison of a Standard Grip (A), a Strickland Offset Thumbhole Grip (B), and the Brunswick Standard Offset Grip (C)

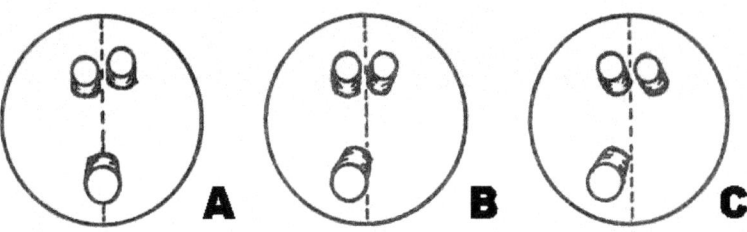

The middle fingerholes of A and B will not feel the same although they are in the same place relative to the centerline. With the standard grip, there is pressure on the bridge side of the first joint (with a fingertip grip); this pressure is relieved by offsetting the thumbhole to a position more in line with the middle fingerhole, such as is shown in B. With C, however, the thumbhole is placed even farther to the left, and the middle fingerhole is pitched 1/16th inch to the right I do not know the reason for this pitch variation. In A, the ring fingerhole is simply drilled parallel with the middle fingerhole to keep them from running together at the bottom. In B, there is a provision for the ring fingerhole to accommodate the direction of flex of that finger, and I have directed it toward the thumb to illustrate this point. This may not be the case with all hands, and this hole may be parallel or even directed slightly away from the middle fingerhole. In C, the ring fingerhole, like the middle fingerhole, is pitched to the right, but only 1/2 inch. Again, I do not know the reason why.

Table 5: The Amount of Weight Removed by the Drilling of Various Hole Sizes – For a comparison of these numbers with those of Bill Taylor and of the AMF Company, see Figure 45. These numbers are well within the limits of accuracy of the beam balance.

Hole Diameters in Inches / Hole Depth in Inches / Weight Removed in Ounces

Hole Dia.	.500	.750	1.000	1.250	1.500	1.750	2.000	2.250	2.500	2.750	3.000
19/32	.119	.178	.238	.297	.356	.416	.475	.534	.594	.653	.713
5/8	.122	.184	.245	.306	.367	.428	.489	.551	.612	.673	.734
21/32	.135	.202	.269	.336	.403	.470	.538	.605	.672	.739	.806
11/16	.148	.222	.296	.369	.443	.517	.591	.665	.739	.813	.887
23/32	.157	.235	.313	.391	.469	.548	.626	.704	.782	.860	.939
3/4	.176	.263	.351	.439	.527	.615	.702	.790	.878	.966	1.054
25/32	.191	.286	.382	.477	.573	.668	.764	.859	.955	1.050	1.146
13/16	.206	.309	.412	.515	.618	.720	.823	.925	1.029	1.132	1.235
27/32	.238	.356	.475	.594	.713	.831	.950	1.068	1.188	1.306	1.425
7/8	.250	.375	.500	.625	.750	.875	1.000	1.125	1.250	1.375	1.500
29/32	.263	.394	.526	.657	.788	.919	1.050	1.182	1.313	1.444	1.576
15/16	.273	.409	.546	.682	.819	.955	1.092	1.228	1.365	1.501	1.638
31/32	.300	.450	.600	.750	.900	1.050	1.200	1.350	1.500	1.650	1.800
1	.325	.488	.650	.813	.975	1.138	1.300	1.463	1.625	1.788	1.950
1-1/32	.350	.525	.700	.875	1.050	1.225	1.400	1.575	1.750	1.925	2.100
1-1/16	.368	.553	.737	.921	1.105	1.289	1.474	1.658	1.842	2.026	2.210
1-3/32	.388	.581	.775	.969	1.163	1.357	1.550	1.744	1.938	2.132	2.326
1-1/8	.400	.600	.800	1.000	1.200	1.400	1.600	1.800	2.000	2.200	2.400
1-5/32	.425	.638	.851	1.063	1.275	1.488	1.700	1.913	2.125	2.338	2.550
1-3/16	.450	.675	.900	1.125	1.350	1.575	1.800	2.025	2.250	2.475	2.700

If one measures the pitch of the fingerholes in relation to the grip layout centerline, lateral pitch will not measure zero (or true zero, as drillers like to say) because they do not lie on a circumferential plane in relation to the centerline plane. When he chooses zero pitches, the driller must not assume that all of the pitches will measure such with a pitch gauge; he must know which pitches are based on the circumference of the ball and which are not. To summarize the three grip versions, the standard grip cramps the hand while too much offset will reduce grip security and promote wobbling of the ball in the swing. Try my version of the offset thumbhole grip and let me know how you like (or dislike) it. The next chapter may show you a better way of fitting the ball you have just drilled.

Table 6: Distance of Shift of the Weight Center Due to Pitch – The center of the weight moves in the direction of pitch.

Pitch in Inches	Hole Depth in Inches										
	.500	.750	1.000	1.250	1.500	1.750	2.000	2.250	2.500	2.750	3.000
1/8	.015	.022	.029	.036	.044	.051	.059	.066	.074	.081	.088
1/4	.028	.043	.058	.073	.088	.103	.118	.133	.148	.163	.178
3/8	.051	.073	.086	.108	.131	.153	.176	.198	.221	.243	.266
1/2	.055	.085	.115	.145	.175	.205	.235	.265	.295	.325	.355
5/8	.069	.106	.144	.181	.219	.256	.294	.331	.369	.406	.444
3/4	.083	.128	.173	.218	.263	.308	.353	.398	.443	.488	.533

Amount of Shift of the Weight Center in Inches

Table 7: Pitch and Bridge Requirements of Some of the Brunswick Patented Grips – Pitches that measure true are marked with an asterisk (*). Ad = adlateral (away from the thumb side of the hand), Ab = ablateral (toward the thumb side of the hand), Lat. = lateral.

Grip Name	Thumb *	Pitch (Inches) Middle Finger	Ring Finger	Bridge
Standard	1/2R, 3/8Ad	5/8F, 9/16Ad	3/8F, 1/2Ad	1/4"
Offset	Offset 1/4"			
Ned Day	1/4F, 1/16Ad	3/8F, 5/8Ad	3/8F, 3/8Ad	3/8"
	No offset			
Marion	1/8F, 1/8Ad	3/8F, 0 lat.	3/8F, 0 lat.	1/4"
Ladewig	No offset			
(Chuck)	0 F/R, 0 lat.	3/8F, 0 lat.	3/8F, 1/16Ab	1/4"
Collier	No offset	*		

I decided to include Table 7 because it may be of interest to younger drillers. According to Lowell Jackson (the actual designer of the Ned Day grip), the Brunswick Corporation patented certain grips for their commercial value of big names, such as Marion Ladewig. The practice subsided during a period of accelerated construction of new establishments when Brunswick de-emphasized the promotion of bowling balls in favor of lanes and related equipment. For more detail concerning patented grips, I refer you to Brunswick's manual #88504; it contains the Connie Schwoegler grip among others. Thanks are due to Mr. James Mailander of the Brunswick Corporation, Skokle, Illinois, for providing me with the information necessary to construct Table 7.

Figure 45: A Graph Showing a Comparison of Weight Removal Figures from Three Different Sources – The figures shown are for a 2-1/2 inch deep hole.

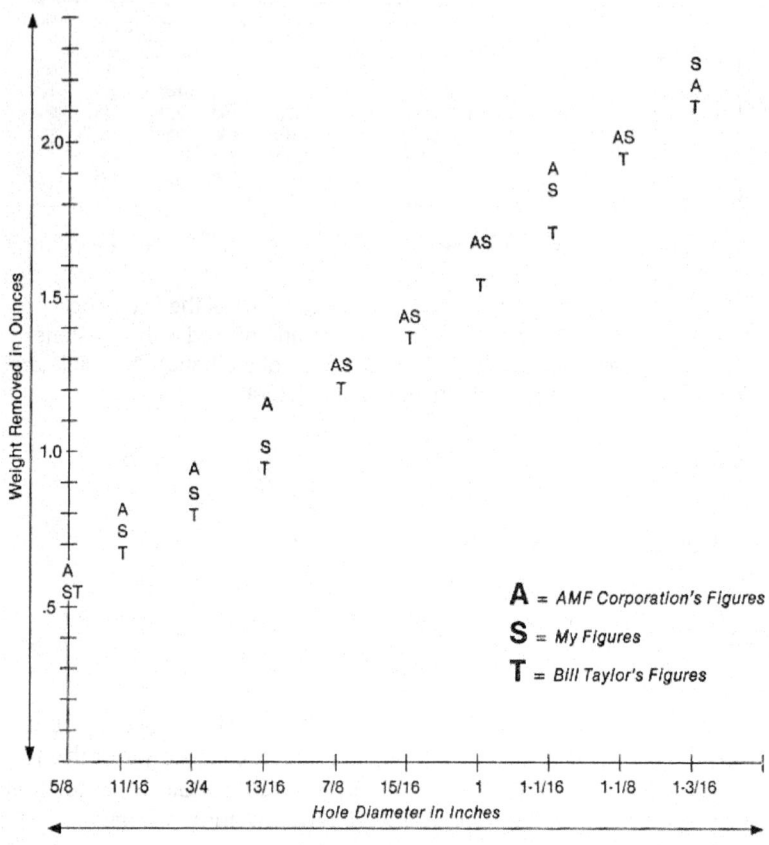

11 Fitting the Drilled Fingertip Grip

I firmly believe that the person who will use the bowling ball should be the one to complete the fitting process — the shaping (contouring) and beveling of the holes. Even though the professional driller may have a lot of expertise, he does not have his customers' nerve endings. By mastering the simple process explained on the following pages and by applying a great deal of concentration to the fingers while they are in the ball (during the fitting process), the bowler can probably obtain a much better fit than any other individual could possibly give him. He will be able to make his own gradual changes in the fit over a longer period of time. During this time, he may bowl several times so he can make a thorough evaluation of each of the small modifications. Such a long-term, trial-and-error process is usually not offered by busy pro shops because they cannot (economically) devote more than one or two hours to fitting a ball for one customer. Occasionally, one finds a pro shop that can give this extra service to its customers; it should be patronized and should enjoy the status of a dependable dentist or optometrist. Most important, the bowler can gain a better (more perceptive) understanding of his needs if he spends some time putting his fingers in the grip and questioning himself about changes in pitch, span, etc. This type of questioning takes a great deal of thought; it simply cannot be done in the one and one half minutes per game period in which the fingers are actually in the grip! The bowler is the only one who can feel the small irregularities of his grip, so the only way to diagnose these problems is for him to learn what to look for.

Goals for Beveling and Shaping the Holes

Although one may not realize it, nearly every area of the fingerhole or thumbhole has a function — it serves some purpose. Each of these areas will be considered in more detail, but first I want to point out some desirable goals of the fitting process. While beveling and shaping the holes, one should strive for:

1. *Preservation of the measured spans and pitches.* The bevel should never extend so far inside the hole that it decreases the span. Likewise, the shaping of the inside of the hole should not change its pitch.

2. *Correct useful size and shape of the holes.* The term useful means that, even though the holes may be correctly contoured (another word for "shaped"), the sizes must accommodate changes in the sizes of the fingers with differences in temperature, humidity, physiology of the bowler, etc. Therefore, there exists an appropriate range within which lie hole size and shape.

3. *A parallel relationship between opposite sides of a hole.* Properly-contoured holes are normally not cylindrical; they are more nearly oval. But further, if there is to be no drag as the thumb and fingers exit the holes, the sidewalls must be parallel with each other — the holes may not be urn-, cone-, or irregularly-shaped.

4. *Smoothness of the entire inner surface of the holes.* If a portion of the skin will slide over an area of the inside of the hole, for minimum abrasion, the sidewalls must be smooth. The gripping surface can be slightly rougher if more traction is desired.

5. *Prevention of the swelling of the thumb.* I recommend the use of an air vent. This is a small (approximately 1/8 inch diameter) hole that allows air to enter the thumbhole as the thumb is withdrawn. This prevents the buildup of moisture and the momentary suction that bunches the skin at the widest part of the thumb. When bunching occurs, the thumb is effectively made too large for its own hole, and abrasion can produce pain and swelling!

Special Considerations of the Fingerholes

Bevel: The beveled portion should be considered a transitional area between the inner surface of the hole and the surface of the ball. As a rule, bevel of the fingerholes of a fingertip grip should never extend more than 3/16 inch into the hole (see Figure 49). Any more can change the pitch. The bevel should be blended so smoothly that there is no visible or detectable difference between the beveled area and the two surfaces. Believe it or not, even the slightest sharpness at the bevel-surface border can cause damage to the skin. As an example, put a grain of salt between the first joints of your bowling fingers and squeeze them together. I bet it is impossible to ignore that tiny grain of salt!

Shaping: The holes should present a more flattened area to the gripping surfaces of the fingers so that the work of lifting is distributed over a larger area. This flatness should be perpendicular to the direction of flex of the fingers (see lines 1 and 2, Figure 46 and Figure 47).

Figure 46: A Bowling Ball with Lines Representing the Directions of Spans Between Thumb and Finger Holes

Figure 47: A Closer Look at the Fingerholes of the Ball Shown in Figure 46, b = the bridge

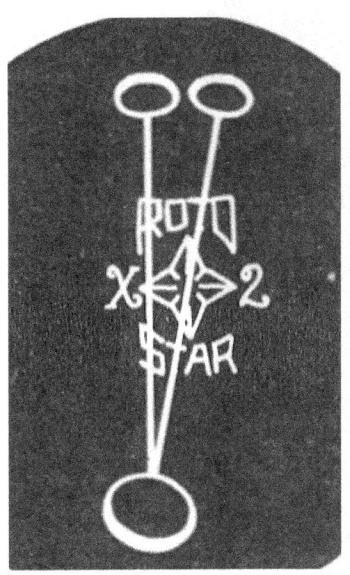
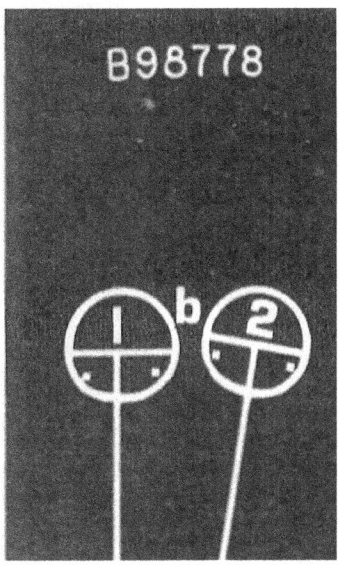

Generally, the width of the hole is determined by both the width of the finger at the first joint and at the level of the edges of the fingernails. If a hole is the ideal shape, the inserted finger stops when the edge of the hole and the inner bend of the knuckle are aligned. Each fingerhole should feel exactly the same to its respective finger, and the edges of the nails should not dig into the surrounding flesh when the grip is made.

Special Considerations of the Thumbhole

Bevel: This is very important and, for explanation, needs to be divided into areas. Figure 46 shows the lines that represent the directions of span on my own rubber ball. Figure 48 is a closer look at the thumbhole of the same ball with the surrounding areas numbered for reference. The holes have been outlined with white paint so they can be seen more clearly in the photograph.

Figure 48: A Closer Look at the Thumbhole of the Ball Shown in Figure 46.

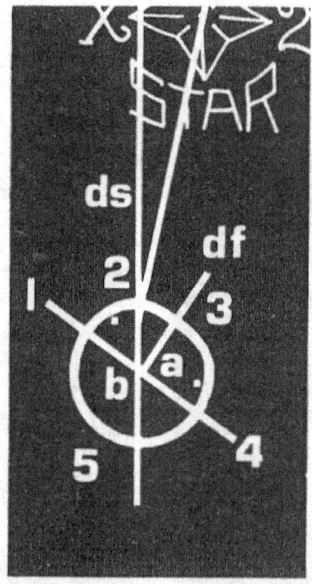

The wide portion of the thumb at the first joint is indicated by the line 1-4. This is almost always perpendicular to the direction of flex of the thumb (angle a), which is labeled df. The letters ds represent the directions of span. Areas 2 and 3 are the portions of the thumbhole

174

bevel that are associated with the directions of span and the direction of flex, respectively. The 1-2-3-4 edge of the hole must be rounded to accommodate the base of the thumb, but it must also be slightly flattened for the gripping face to slide over as it clears the hole. This double requirement presents a problem, and therefore, *bevel (as well as the shaping of the hole) of the 1-2-3-4 area must be a compromise of both needs.* Area 5, or the back of the hole, is the portion that regulates the depth to which the thumb can be inserted. Too little bevel can result in a less-than-secure grip because the thumb cannot be inserted far enough; too much bevel can allow the thumb to be inserted too far, and a callous can develop on the palm of the hand at the base of the thumb. Refer again to Figure 49.

Shaping: The hole must be wider than thick to accommodate the width of the thumb at the first joint. It should never be so loose that it allows bending or knuckling of the thumb to occur, but *the hole should never be so tight that it prohibits the slight turn of the thumb as it is clearing the hole.* This turn is necessary if any horizontal rotation is imparted by the hand at the release point.

If the contour is at the proper angle (the angle formed by the direction of span of the middle fingerhole and line 1-4 — angle b), there should be no drag as the grip is tried. The shape and size of the thumbhole can be appropriate, but if the angle of the contour is off, the thumb can drag. If the angle is correct, the thumbhole seems to be its largest when the fingers and thumb are inserted simultaneously. This is why it is important to test any progress of shaping the thumbhole only while the fingers are fully inserted in their holes; the proper relationship is then maintained.

Instructions for Beveling and Shaping the Holes

Before reading the stepwise procedure in finishing the fitting of the ball, please familiarize yourself with the material presented in Figure 49 and Figure 50. Figure 49, diagram A presents some terminology concerning bevel (A). Note that bevel should always be applied at a 45 degree angle to the surface of the hole. The width of the bevel is measured from the ball surface to the inner surface of the hole. Diagram B shows two improper bevel types, and diagram C shows

175

four ways in which a hole can be improperly contoured. These are usually the result of using a bevel sander.

Figure 49: A. Bevel Terminology: L = light, M = moderate, H = heavy, VH = very heavy. B. Improper Bevel Types: The angle of the bevel is other than 45 degrees to the surface of the ball. C. Improper Shaping of the Hole: 1. the cone-shaped hole, 2. the urn-shaped hole, 3. and 4. irregularly-shaped holes

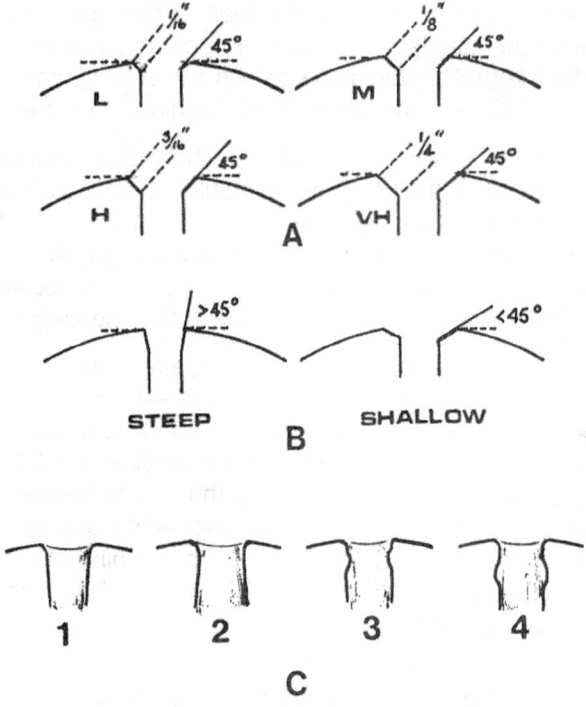

Figure 50 is a picture of some of the equipment that I use and recommend for fitting any grip. A is white rubbing compound, B is a variable-speed, reversible electric drill that is used in conjunction with the drills, E (1/8 inch diameter) and F (5/32 inch diameter), to make the air vent, or with the pointed grinding stone (D) to apply a starting bevel. C is the all-important hobbyist's drill (often called a "Moto-Tool"). When used with a variable speed control like T (one I made for $5 using a light dimmer switch), it is the most versatile of all bowling shop tools. O is a group of barrel or drum sanding attachments; P is a pair of useful rounded steel cutters used for

Figure 50: Recommended Tools for the Beveling and Shaping of the Holes in a Bowling Ball)

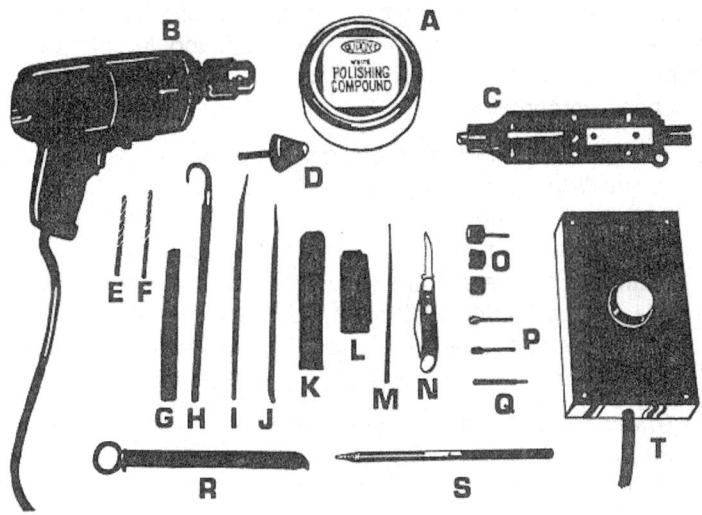

shaping small areas. Q is a portion of chain saw sharpening rasp — the best beveling instrument I have ever used. It is far superior to the three-cornered knife that requires constant sharpening. The rasp never needs sharpening, and even an old one works amazingly well. Q has been ground down so it will fit into the hobbyist's drill; it was broken off of the rasp M, which I use for more exacting applications. G is Red Devil Dragon Skin, a metal grater that is useful for removing large amounts of material. H, I, and J are round files in decreasing order of coarseness. They are necessary for shaping. The curve of H is for securing a grip with the little finger; the bend of I was accidental; and the bend of J is for use in hard-to-reach areas at the bottom of holes. K and L are coarse and fine emery cloth, respectively, and N is a plain pocket knife that is used to smooth the bevel. R is a flexible steel span scale and S is a wax pencil; they are included because I had mentioned them in the previous chapter and because they are used to mark the ball prior to shaping. Please take a few moments to study these two figures so you understand them before proceeding.

Before reading the stepwise procedure, keep these points in mind. First, take out enough material from the holes, but avoid removing too much at one time; the fitting process probably will continue over a period of days to uncover problems that are detectable while bowling with the ball. Second, trim and file callouses before attempting to fit any ball; do not attempt to fit a ball to swollen, sore, injured, or moist hands — the holes will invariably be made too large! Use the following sequence of steps when fitting a bowling ball; vacuum the holes when appropriate:

1. **Apply a light bevel to the fingerholes and a moderate bevel to the thumbhole.** The best method is to use a fine rasp on the edges of the holes while the ball is being rotated on a mechanical turntable (similar to a potter's wheel). An alternate method is to use a drum sander or round rasp in a hobbyist's drill that is turning at low speed. With either method, one should blend the bevel with a knife and finish it off with fine sandpaper.

   Unacceptable Method: Never use a bevel sander for beveling the holes or shaping the holes! Take a closer look at Figure 49, C. Diagram 1 shows what happens if the bevel sander is held too long at the top of the hole; diagram 2 shows what happens if the sander is held too long at the bottom. In diagrams 3 and 4, the bevel sander may have been uniformly run up-and-down inside the hole, but different hardnesses of materials in the core, weight block, and shell have been removed in different amounts. The bigger the hole in a certain area, the softer the material at that level. In the case of the urn and cone-shaped holes, the driller is at fault; in the cases represented by diagrams 3 and 4, however, the errors may not be avoidable by the driller. These are the reasons that I am opposed to the use of the bevel sander on a newly-drilled grip. The instrument is fine for preparing holes prior to plugging, but that is the extent of its usefulness. The speed and the sanding area are not controlled, therefore, the hole can be made too large too quickly. The pitch of the hole can be altered if the sander is not perfectly parallel with the pitch when it is being inserted and withdrawn from the hole. Likewise, the sander can score the holes thereby creating a more abrasive surface that must be removed by additional sanding. In short, it is fast but inaccurate. Use a drum sander instead.

2. **Mark the fingerholes with a wax pencil at the widest points of the fingers.** See Figure 47. The marks should coincide with the ends of the lines labeled 1 and 2. These lines are perpendicular to the directions of flex in this example (remember that my ring finger flexes toward the thumb).

3. **Shape the fingerholes so that the fingers fit as described in the section "Special Considerations of the Fingerholes."** Remove material from the areas adjacent to the small squares in the photograph. Use a drum sander, Dragon Skin, and/or a coarse rat tail file if there is much material to be removed. Use a finer rasp and/or coarse emery cloth if there is less material to remove. Use finer emery cloth and/or a fine rasp if little material must be removed. Remember, you can't put material back in once you have taken it out! Here are some of the recommended movements to be used with certain tools:

   a. Drum sander – up-and-down (inside the hole), side-to-side
   b. Steel shaping bit – up-and-down and side-to-side, i. e. a circular motion
   c. Dragon Skin – up-and-down only
   d. Files, rasp – a rolling motion
   e. Emery cloth – up-and-down only

4. **Restore the bevel to those areas that were shaped.** The same bevel should exist around the entire edge of the hole. It looks better, and there should not be much bevel anyway!

5. **Before moving on to the thumbhole, drill the air vent.** Use the electric drill (the hobbyist's drill does not have enough torque) with a 1/8 inch or a 5/32 inch drill bit. In your imagination, extend the ds span line of the middle finger to a point one inch to one and one-half inches below the thumbhole. Rest the tip of the drill at this point, and, while looking into the thumbhole, drill this air vent so that it enters the thumbhole somewhere near the bottom. While bowling, the air vent exit hole should not contact the thumb, because it can cause abrasion itself. Drilling this hole before further contouring the thumbhole minimizes the chances of removing too much material.

6. **Insert the fingers to the proper depth and insert the thumb to the first joint only. Mark the ball at the widest point of the first joint (Line 1-4,** Figure 48. **Insert the thumb all of**

179

the way (as soon as possible — it may not be possible until the hole is partially shaped) and mark the direction of flex (df). Also mark the ball at the back of the hole (the position of the thumb bone, Area 5)

7. **Shape the thumbhole at the areas indicated by the marks.** Keep in mind the goals stated in "Special Considerations of the Thumbhole." Preserve the span at area 2 (Figure 48), and remove material in the regions adjacent to the small squares in the photograph. This gives the desired flatness of the beveled area, while preserving the roundness for the base of the thumb. Follow step 3, a-e.

8. **Restore the bevel to the shaped areas.** Blend the bevel with a knife, and finish with fine emery cloth.

9. **Finish the interior surfaces of the holes with fine, dry sandpaper or Crocus Cloth.** Leave the gripping surfaces a little rougher, if desired.

10. **Vacuum the holes and clean them with a little rubbing alcohol or lighter fluid.** Do not use a water-based cleaner.

11. **Rub the inside of the holes with skin oil obtained from the outer ear (not the wax), the forehead, or from the sides of the nose.** Do not use powder, because it tends to trap moisture in the hole and promote abrasion.

12. **Try the ball by bowling with it.** Repeat any steps necessary but never omit steps 9, 10, and 11.

Even with the best grip, it sometimes is not possible to get a firm hold on the ball. This can be due to humidity and to perspiration. In my case, I find it difficult to hold onto a plastic ball. To solve this problem, I have found a very fine cloth tape. it can be torn by hand, and the adhesive is substantial enough to allow several trials of placing the strip into the hole. I highly recommend it; it is sold under the name of Super Tuftex All-Purpose Tape and is available from the Becker Davison Corporation, Seattle, Washington 98134, in a wide variety of widths and colors. It is often necessary to make the holes effectively smaller. This can be accomplished by applying vinyl tape in the hole surfaces opposite the gripping surfaces. Several thicknesses can be made, cut, and inserted in to the hole, and one thickness at a time can be removed as the thumb or fingers become larger. Two companies that manufacture this type of tape are 3M (Scotch) and

Mystic. Remember, few tapes or grip adhesives can withstand the summer temperatures in the trunk of a car.

Even after the holes have been sanded, smoothed and conditioned properly, abrasion is always a possibility — especially during the trial period of a new ball. If it is suspected that certain parts of the thumb or fingers will develop blisters, one may try to prevent their formation by putting some flexible collodion (New Skin, court plaster, etc.) on those areas before bowling. Even better is the new "super" glue (cyanoacrylate base). Do not put this on an open sore, however, unless you want to jump through the ceiling! After blisters form, cotton and flexible collodion may have to be used, but this is not a cure or a relief from pain — just a compensation.

A Final Word

Don't be disappointed if your enthusiasm is met with indifference I have experienced such a negative reaction from critics. These are the persons who do not want to take the time necessary to carry out the procedure even when they know nothing about it! With the proper tools it really doesn't take very long, and, if you are a professional driller, the customer whom you properly fit with a grip will be a friend. If you are fitting yourself using this procedure, you won't believe how good a properly-fitted grip can be. As for the skeptics, I feel sorry for them because they will never know the difference. As is said, "Ignorance is its own punishment!"

Recommended Reading

As I have stated repeatedly in this book, one must learn as much as he can in order to grow intellectually. Even though I cannot dispute the fact that a person may become a fine bowler without ever having read about the sport; I think he is missing much of the enjoyment. The following is an annotated list of some books that I have had the pleasure to read.

Omission from the list does not indicate that I disapprove of a book, and I must apologize to those authors of fine texts that I have not listed. Naturally I do not agree with every opinion written in these books, but I do not necessarily disagree with all of them either. Likewise, I do not expect everyone to agree with every one of mine, although I have taken great care to explain the reasoning behind them. This disagreement is the very essence of what can make you a more intelligent bowler — you can read and judge for yourself!

Professional Bowlers Association Guide to Better Bowling written by Chuck Pezzano and published by Simon and Schuster. This book includes a section of tips from touring PBA members. Also interesting is the listing of PBA statistics.

The Secret of Bowling Strikes written by Dawson Taylor and published by Wilshire Book Company. Originally written in 1960 by a Detroit automobile dealer presently with the National Enquirer, this book contains previously unwritten techniques that were used by the great bowlers of the '20s, '30s and '40s to improve their games. Taylor did an excellent job of explaining valuable off-the-lane methods such as the use of the metronome to improve timing, the use of a strip of adhesive tape on the floor to straighten the approach, and the use of a small rubber squeeze ball to strengthen the finger muscles. He explains the explosion point in detail and tells the strategy that should be used in league play. None of these concepts had been discussed in one work before, and the book is a most helpful introductory book on the strength of these concepts that are still omitted from most beginning instruction manuals.

Bowling for All written by Joe Falcaro and Murray Goodman and published by Ronald Press. This is an old publication that has been revised twice, the last revision being in 1966. Because of its style and illustrations, it is entertaining. Half of the book is ABC rules and schedules for team play.

Bowling written by Norman E. Showers and published by Goodyear Publishing Company. Specifically a college text written by a professional educator, this book contains a very complete treatment of beginning concepts and more advanced concepts as beginning students would be expected to understand them. Particularly interesting is Showers' systematic treatment of common faults, their symptoms, and some of their common remedies. At the back of the book are instructional objectives that list various characteristics of the delivery. Both of these sections provide effective starting outlines for anyone planning a self-improvement program.

Bowling – Fencing Guide written as a compilation of various articles by many authors and published by The Division for Girls' and Womens' Sports; The American Association for Health, Physical Education and Recreation. I included this book because it contains lists of selected research papers, sources of materials, and bibliographies. These items are not usually a part of bowling instruction manuals. Contributors to this collection of articles are amateur bowlers who are professional educators and who are involved in some facet of bowling instruction such as for the handicapped, motor learning skills, psychology, and statistics. It is interesting to note that students have received Master of Science and Doctor of Philosophy degrees for their work on various aspects of bowling. Most of these studies are not relevant to bowlers of high proficiency, but they do serve to illustrate that some official accreditation is given for detailed studies of the sport.

Ten Secrets of Bowling written by Don Carter and Anthony Ravielli and published by Viking Press. This presents a plane analysis of Don Carter's delivery through a series of fine drawings by Ravielli. The commentary about each facet of the delivery is written so that Carter seems to be speaking to the reader. I have not seen any other publication like this, and I hope that it is not the last.

The Complete Guide to Better Bowling written by several contributors and edited by Howard J. Lewis and published by the Maco Magazine Company. This includes, in addition to fine articles on technique, many excellent pictures of Brunswick stars. There is an impressive question-and-answer section written by Joe Norris, and a chapter that relates many interesting stories of the personalities and events of the American Bowling Congress tournaments.

Bowling Tips from Brunswick Stars written by many contributors, edited by Robert Strain Spiess, and published by Fawcett Publications. Twenty-two Brunswick staff members relate their own personal bowling strategies through a series of pictures and easy-to-read commentary. These people are some of my favorite personalities, and I recommend this book to anyone who wishes to learn more about them.

Better Bowling written by Joe Wilman and published by the Ronald Press Company. A basic book written with humor as well as insight, this was the first bowling text I ever read. I think it should be the first text for the beginning bowler also, because of its completeness and clarity. Wilman was long known as an excellent bowling teacher, and this book is a credit to his reputation.

The Bowler's Manual written by Lou Bellisimo and published by Prentice-Hall Incorporated. Originally written as a guide for college and high school teachers, this has become the most widely-used text for students taking bowling for course credit. A fine bowler and gentleman, Bellisimo taught bowling at the University of Oregon for several years, and this is where material was developed for the book. He details the "one-step" delivery for correcting problems, and the book is almost entirely devoted to the approach and delivery, leaving (rightly so) redundant instructions on how to keep score etc., to less useful texts.

AMF Guide to Natural Bowling written by Victor Kalman with the assistance of 36 AMF staff members and published by Pocket Books Incorporated. This is a basic text without photographs. The text is written in a reporting style, and it contains much information. The organization of the book is very effective, and the "Clinic" section is superb. It suffers, however, from the absence of photographs in chapters that deal with the approach and various hand positions.

185

The Secrets of the Stars written by members of the Brunswick advisory staff and published by the Brunswick Corporation. This is really a pamphlet that was usually given free to the customer who purchased a new Brunswick ball. It is probably the most quoted and copied publication of any concerned with the sport, there being entire sections of it found in numerous other method books. It is a handsome little book, and older copies are certain to be collectors' items someday.

Inside Bowling written by Don Johnson and published by the Henry Regnery Company. Written in a very personal style by a colorful bowler, this book contains many comments never before found in beginning bowling texts. Johnson deals with characteristics of the bowling ball in some detail, and a chapter is devoted to attitude. Technique is discussed thoroughly. I recommend this book as a second step for the aspiring bowler.

How You Can Bowl Better Using Self-hypnosis written by Jack Heise and published by Wilshire Press. Without reservation, I can say that this book is an absolute necessity to the bowler. Every other author talks about how something feels, but Heise is the only one who really explains the concept. He shows the bowler how to incorporate good habits and eliminate bad ones through self-hypnosis. With the aid of Brunswick champions, Heise develops his theme in a very systematic, simple manner that can be understood by the youngest aspiring bowler. I use the principles outlined in the book, and I can attest to their effectiveness.

How to Bowl Better written by Ned Day and published by Fawcett Publications. Originally written in 1948, this book was one of the most thorough of its day. Even now, the book says more about the delivery than most new texts. Ned Day was the idol of many of the great bowlers of the '50s and '60s, and the book has excerpts from the RKO-Pathe film, "Strikes to Spare" that shows his classic approach.

Balance written by Bill Taylor and available from Western Columbia or from BT Bowling Products. This is a long overdue treatise on Taylor's concepts of weight distribution within bowling balls and how this relates to the followthrough, to the type of track, and to the action of the ball on the lane. The text is involved, but it is not really difficult for the serious reader. I agree strongly with Taylor in that a good amount of detail is necessary to thoroughly explain a topic. The book is "too technical only for those who do not have enough interest to put forth the effort necessary to understand the author's explanations.

Add 30 Pins to Your Bowling Score by Billy Welu with Jerry Levine
This book is another excellent beginning-to-intermediate text, and the writing style reflects the author's sense of humor and unique way with words. As many do not know, besides being a champion bowler, Welu had completed graduate study in psychology, and his articulate chapter devoted to bowling psychology is an excellent one. However, the best portion of the book includes his chapters on lane conditions and parallel line bowling. These should be thoroughly studied, and the principles practiced consistently. They will improve the accuracy of anyone, regardless of average.

Glossary

Abduction (of the hand): contraction of muscles in the area of the wrist that move the hand in the direction of the thumb.

Aberrant Swing: an armswing that deviates from a perfectly parallel relationship with the body's centerline plane. It can be convergent with or divergent from the approach line.

Ablateral (pitch): pitch of fingerholes or the thumbhole that is directed away from the geometric center of the ball and toward the thumb side of the hand.

Adaptive Range: the array or complement of skills that a bowler possesses that allow him to score consistently close to the maximum scoring potential on a variety of different lane conditions.

Adduction (of the hand): contraction of muscles In the area of the wrist that move the hand in a direction away from the thumb.

Approach Line: the path of the steps on the approach that correspond to a desired target line. It is closely followed by the center of gravity of the body during the approach.

Axis of Rotation: the axis of the track on the surface of the ball. It is 180-degrees opposed to the plane of the track.

Bevel: the removal of the sharp edges of drilled fingerholes or thumbhole.

Blocking: selective application of dressing to or the selective sanding of the lane surface in an effort to guide the ball into the strike pocket.

Break Point: the place along the target line where the ball begins to hook.

Bridge (web): the area between the near edges of two adjacent fingerholes.

Centerline: a segment of the Great Circle (circumference) of a ball upon which the grip is to be superimposed.

Centerline Plane of the Body: a plane that divides the body into right and left halves and that intersects the body's center of gravity.

Convergent Swing: an armswing, the plane of which would cross the approach line if both were extended in front of the bowler.

Divergent Swing: an armswing, the plane of which would deviate away from the approach line if both were extended in front of the bowler.

Drift: deviation of the footwork from a desired approach line.

Drift Compensation Factor: the number of boards or inches that the stance position is adjusted to compensate for drift.

Durometer: a device, equipped with a needle and a gauge, designed to measure the hardness of materials. Readings reflect the ability of the needle to penetrate the surface of the material when a constant pressure is applied.

Explosion Point: the instant in which the fingers lift the ball onto the lane surface.

Extension: the lengthening of a limb or extremity, i. e. muscle contraction brings about motion away from the body's centerline plane.

Flexion: the shortening of a limb or extremity, i. e. muscle contraction generally brings about motion toward the body's centerline plane.

Followthrough: continuation of the swing after release of the ball.

Forward Pitch: direction of the axis of a fingerhole or thumbhole away from the geometric center of the ball and toward the opposite hole or set of holes.

Foul Line Correction: see Subconscious Correction, below.

Full Roller: a ball bearing a track that is equal to the circumference of the ball itself. The track usually passes over the area between the fingerholes and the thumbhole.

Geometrics: measurement of the spatial relationships among various points on a surface of or within an object.

Grip: the means with which the hand grasps the bowling ball.

Horizontal Rotation: a turning motion applied to the ball by the hand at the release point.

Instinctive Bowler: sometimes called an area bowler; actually a misnomer; applies to an accomplished bowler whose alignment is of such good quality that his accuracy really does not heavily depend on his fixing his gaze on a small, specific target point.

Kinesiology: the study of human motion, including muscle contraction, flexion and extension of extremities, and the coordination of all such movements.

Kinetic Chain: a sequence of coordinated movements that accomplish a desired result.

Leverage: as it applies to bowling; power gained by the effective use of body mass and motion.

Line: that which connects two points on the surface of an object.

Offset (fingerhole or thumbhole): holes that are drilled off of the grip layout centerline.

Perception: awareness of the environment through observation as well as understanding.

Pitch: the degree of directness of the axis of a hole toward or away from the geometric center of the ball.

Placement Distance: the distance, in board widths or inches, between the approach line and the target line. It reflects the distance between the center of the sliding foot and the board upon which the ball contacts the lane at the release.

Plane: an imaginary entity that cuts through an object in an analogous fashion to a knife slicing through a wedge of cheese.

Pocket: squarely between the 1 and 3 pins for a right-handed bowler and between the 1 and 2 pins for a left-handed bowler; usually 17 boards from the channel on each side.

Rangefinder: the name used to describe the combination of dots and arrows inlaid on the modern bowling lane and approach. It was given that name by Brunswick because of analogy to the sights on a rifle.

Relaxation: as it applies to sports activities; the minimum degree of muscle contraction necessary to perform a task.

Release Correction: see Subconscious Correction, below.

Reverse Pitch: direction of the axis of a fingerhole or thumbhole away from the geometric center of the ball and away from the opposite hole or set of holes.

Semiroller: a ball bearing a track that is approximately 2/3 of the circumference of the ball or greater, but less than that of the Full Roller.

Semispinner: a ball bearing a track that is less than approximately 2/3 of the circumference of the ball.

Shaping: the contouring of the drilled holes to accommodate the proportions of the fingers or thumb.

Shot: the method employed by the bowler to hit the pocket and strike; also refers to the method that is favored by a particular lane condition.

Span: the distance between the near edges of a fingerhole and the thumbhole.

Spot: the term, correctly used, that denotes the place where a bowler fixes his gaze during the approach only if that place is where the ball makes initial contact with the lane surface. Incorrectly used, it has come to mean any place where the ball is to be aimed on the lane. See Spot Bowler, below.

Spot Bowler: a non-existent bowler whose skill is so great that he can strike by standing anywhere on the approach and rolling the ball over any spot he chooses.

Stance: the body position on the approach at the beginning of the delivery. (***Author's Note:*** Today this is called the setup.)

Subconscious Correction: actually a misnomer applies to a compensation that has been mechanically induced by errors in the delivery. It usually results in bringing the ball closer to the pocket area when the target line has been missed. It is more obvious on blocked lanes and has been tagged a correction, thus giving the bowler to which this happens more credit than he deserves.

Summation of Internal Forces: a general term that describes the performance of any sport skill. It consists of the preparation phase (the stance), the movement phase (the approach), and the followthrough.

Surface Properties: the hardness, color, or frictional characteristics of the surface of a bowling ball or bowling lane.

Swing Compensation Factor: the number or boards or inches that the stance position is adjusted to compensate for an aberrant swing.

Target Line: the desired trajectory of the ball toward a particular target. It is sometimes called a playing angle and is usually named by the board numbers of two points that it crosses — the point of ball contact with the lane (the foul line point) and the point at which the ball crosses the level of the arrows (the arrow level point).

Target Point: any place along, or very close to, the target line and upon which the bowler fixes his gaze during the approach and delivery.

Targeting System: the method by which the body is aligned in an effort to direct the ball to a desired target.

Too Technical: a term used by persons who do not understand a concept in an effort to avoid having to explain it, as in "Now, I don't want to get too technical...."

Track (on the ball): the area of the ball that contacts the lane.

Track (on the lane): the area, usually to the right of center, that is worn to a greater extent than other areas.

Vertical Rotation: a lifting motion applied to the ball by the hand at the release point.

Weight Block: a compact mass of dense material placed roughly between the core and the shell of a bowling ball and intended to create a difference in weight between top and bottom halves.

Weight Center Shift: movement of the center of gravity of a bowling ball away from the geometric center of the grip.

Index

Numerics

3M (Scotch) Company 180

A

abduction 17
ablateral pitch 43
ablateral thumbhole pitch 50
Ace Bowling Balls 114
adaptive range
    building 137
    effective 129
    increasing 127
    outside one's 128
    synthetic-lane bowler 155
adduction of the wrist 17, 60
adlateral pitch 43
adlateral thumbhole pitch 50
air 172
air vent in thumbhole 172
alignment
    body planes 57
    centerline 164
    chin-knee-foot 57
    grip centerline 60
    learned by professionals 65
    long plane of bowling arm .. 57
    planes 133
    swing 146
Allison, Glenn 26
Amburgey Bowling Balls 115
Amburgey, J. D. 103
American Broadcasting
    Company 11
AMF Bowling Balls 114, 121
angle of attack 77, 127, 153
approach line

converging with target line . 90
    deviating from desired 68
    diverges from target line 90
    extreme inside lines 93
    parallel with target line 68
    straightaway lines 93
    vs. target line 76
arm
    construction 17
    movements 17
arrow level point
    defined 76
    moving 86
    spares 99
automatic movements 20
away pitch (ablateral) 42
axis
    full roller 113
    loading 117
    of rotation 17, 111
    weighted ball 105

B

bag of shots 127, 130
balance
    dynamic 119
    static 119
ball path error 74
ball speed
    increasing 136
    lower on urethane finishes 61
Barrett, Les 53
Basic H (Shaklee) 125
beam balance
    reference manuals 118
    static weight 116
    top weight 112
beam balance error 118
Bellisimo, Lou 53, 149, 185
bevel sander 37
beveling
    considerations 173
    goals 172

holes 171
instructions 175
tools 177
blisters, treating 181
block specialist 85
body planes alignment 57
Bomar, Buddy 70, 88
bottom weight 110, 140
bowling ball
   bottom weight 110, 140
   cleanliness 125, 140, 141
   construction 105
   core-dense 103
   degreasing 125
   high RG 103
   improper fit 20
   inaccurate fitting 32
   loading 117
   low RG 103
   researchers 103
   shell-dense 103
   steps in manufacture 106
   twelve measurements 23
   visual perspectives 40
   weighing 118
   weight center shift 106
bowling glove 47
break point 70, 76, 77
bridge
   Brunswick grips 169
   defined 23
   general considerations 24
   pressure on first joint 167
   too wide 24
Brunswick
   advisory staff 186
   bowling stars 185
   Edge 121
   Fireball 124
   Gil-Mac 32
   LT-48 121
   offset thumbhole grip 28
   patented grips 169
   puddle weight block 114

Rangefinder 70
Starfire 124
Bunetta, Bill 50

C

callouses
   in new areas 48
   thumb 48
   trim and file 178
   unnecessary 20
Carter, Don 184
Celucoat 144
cement, Pliobond 62
center of gravity 103, 189, 190, 193
centerline
   alignment in ball cradle 164
   defined 25
   thumbhole starting position 47
centripetal force 64
characteristics
   altering ball 129
   ball roll 24, 103
   bodily 77
   bowling ball 108, 140, 154
   cover 126
   delivery 54, 154
   hand 45
   human 15
   inanimate 15
   machine tools 32
   non-variable 151
   swing 85
   variable 6, 140
Chic Grip 27
Childers, W. J. "Red" 105
cleanliness of ball 125, 140, 141
clockface terminology 29, 39
Collier grip 26
collodion 181
Columbia
   300 Caramel 124
   300 yellow dot 121

Columbia Bowling balls 114
conventional grip 26
   load sharing of fingers 37
   precautions 46
   starting fingerhole size 38
   weight removed by holes . 109
convergent swing 91
court plaster 181
crankers 82
crocus cloth 180
cupped wrist 17, 60

D

Day, Ned 169, 186
degreasing ball 125
delivery
   adjustment of variables 148
   babying the shot 61
   characteristics ... 54, 132, 154
   elements 54
   foul line body position 56
   fudging the shot 61
   one-step 185
   role of leverage 53
   spot bowler 75
   subconscious mechanics ... 20
   target point 88
direction of flex 48
direction of span 48, 174
divergent swing 92
dot/arrow targeting system ... 67
Dragon Skin 179
drift
   away from target line 95
   compensation 92
   defined 92
   determining cause 95
   direction 92
   personal pattern 101
   toward target line 95
drill press 24
   AMF 32
   Gil-Mac 32

standard 32
straight (standard) 33
drilling
   extra hole 117
   importance of accuracy 33
   instructions 162
   machine 32
   off-center 106
durometer
   calibrate before using 162
   error 123
   hard rubber ball 151
   influence of temperature .. 123
dynamic
   analysis 119
   balance 119
   ball motion 103
   extra holes 117
   weight center depth 116

E

Easter, Ebber "Sarge" 27
Ebonite
   drilling manual 49
   Emerald 300 124
   Magnum 10 121
Ebonite Bowling Balls 114
energy transfer
   broken at wrist 60
   link 57
   max with minimum effort ... 57
   shoulder to fingers 60
error
   ball path 74
   beam balance 118
   fitting spans 23, 36
   footwork path 93
   hardness measurement ... 123
   swing plane 90
   weight calculations 112
explosion point ... 20, 45, 55, 60

197

F

Falcaro, Joe 184
files
  bevel and shaping tools .. 177
  proper motion 179
finesse shot 148
finger weight
  grip layout centerline 164
  later hook 107, 141
  removal of ball material ... 110
  Roto-Star balls 104
  synthetic lane 156
  thumb weight tradeoff 140
fingerhole pitch
  correct feel 46
  wide span 45
fingers
  direction of flex 48
  inserts 37
  muscles 43
  tip-to-elbow plane 47
fingertip grip
  bevel of fingerholes 173
  described 28
  fingers share the load 35
  inserting fingers 35
  pressure on bridge side ... 167
  proper span appearance ... 36
  proper starting hole size 38
  relaxed 36
  span error 23
  span goal 45
  stretch 35
  vs. semifingertip grip 27
  vs. two-finger grip 25
flat swing 55
flex
  changing amount of wrist 132
  direction of 43, 50
  direction of ring finger 46
  fingers 18, 55
  incorrect direction 47
  middle finger 44
  ring finger 45

thumb 48
flexed wrist 17
flexion-extension 17, 60
Flores, Al 31
followthrough
  ease of extension 74
  less than 90 degrees 83
  speed 55, 133
footwork
  cadence 133
  error in path 93
  speed vs. length of swing 133
forward pitch
  arch of fingers 35
  excessive in thumbhole 49
  less in ring fingerhole 46
  middle fingerhole 29
  more lift 141
  opposite of reverse pitch 41
  thumbhole 48
foul line
  balance at finish 54
  body position 56
  lane track 25
  near-in target 75
  point 76, 86, 96
full roller
  different from semi-roller ..107
  long skid 113
  Randolph Classic ball 114

G

Gengler, Count 25
geometric center 23, 25
  pitch relative to 41
  relative to weight center ...115
  zero pitch 39
geometrics 65
Gil-Mac 32
glove, padded bowling ... 47, 62
Golembiewski, Billy 27
Goodman, Murray 184
Goodyear Pliobond cement ..62

gravity 63, 103
grip
  achieving power 19
  bridge 164
  Brunswick offset thumbhole ...
    28
  Brunswick patented 169
  centerline alignment 60
  Chic 27
  Collier 26
  comfort 24
  Connie Schwoegler 169
  conventional 26
  conventional, turn potential 27
  cork 61
  desirable goal 18
  effortless power 43
  fingertip 23, 28, 35
  imperfect fit 20
  kinesiologically sound 30
  layout centerline 25, 40
  measurement sheet .. 22, 162
  relaxation 19
  Sarge Easter 27
  semifingertip 27
  semifingertip, turn potential 27
  standard fingertip 27
  stretching spans 18, 23
  Strickland offset thumbhole 28
  two-finger 25
gripping face
  thumb 48, 175
gripping surface of thumb 47
grips
  cork 61
  rubber 61

H

hand
  action in passing the foot . 134
  adjust position 79
  ball forces adduction 58
  centripetal force 64
  changing position 134
  characteristics 45

construction 17
exercise before fitting 24
flexibility 36
flexion/extension at wrist . 134
hollow vs. padded glove ...47,
  62
movements 17
muscles 18
position and ball speed 138
semifingertip grip 27
stress points 59, 60
  vs. Brunswick offset thumb-
    hole grip 28
hardness 151
  ball material 178
  cover of ball 122, 141
  dry lanes 151
  enforcement problems 123
  enforcing rules 123
  goal of choosing 148
  high 114
  low 122
  measure before weighing 162
  PBA lower limit 122
  playing lanes 151
  reliable testing 123
  standardized in testing 108
  vs. skid and hook 141
Heise, Jack 20, 159, 186
hole size
  criteria 37
  fitting 37
  general considerations 24
  weight removal 168
  weight shift 110
hypnosis of self 20, 159, 186

I

imbalance
  body in stance 54
  calculating 163
  drilling to create 106
  dynamic analysis 119
  illegal 117
  loading a bowling ball 117

199

predicting location 103
  surface properties 108
inserts 37
instinctive bowling 157

J

Jackson, Lowell 70, 169
Johnson, Don 186

K

kinetic chain 56, 191
King, Johnny 27

L

lacquer lane finish 113, 143, 145
Ladewig, Marion 169
lane condition
  adapting to 67, 86, 130
  blocked 145
  bowler versatility 65
  dry 154
  full roller 113
  hook size varies 70
  ideal 67, 143
  influences target line 67
  lousy 128
  neglected 149
  new emerging 14
  oil-soaked 152
  one ball insufficient 13
  soaker ball 122
  synthetic 155
  unfair blocking 85
  various angles 76
lane playing (see target line) 65
leaves
  strong 138
  tight pocket 154
  weak 139
leverage
  body position 56

clean release 133
fingerhole pitch 24
grip 57
  loss 139
  maximum 53
  plane alignment 60
  release 31
  semifingertip grip 27
Levine, Jerry 187
Lillard, Bill 26, 70
Lind shoes 63
Lindemann, Tony 158
line
  approach 68
  bowling vs. spot bowling 66
  foul 25, 54, 75
  imaginary 40
  parallel 53, 65
  perpendicular 53
  target 57, 67
  two-dimensional 40
line vs. plane 40
load
  distribution 36
  sharing, fingers 35, 58
  sharing, wrist supports 62
loading a bowling ball 117
Lubanski, Ed 25, 27

M

Mailander, James 169
Maltz, Maxwell 159
Manhattan
  Green Pea 124
Manhattan Bowling Balls 114
measurement
  bridge 23
  cause and effect 156
  hardness 124
  lateral thumbhole pitch 50
  pitches 23
  sheet 22
  spans 23

thumbhole pitch 49
MEK (methyl ethyl ketone) .. 122
mental framework 6
methyl ethyl ketone (MEK) .. 122
Mitchell, Ace 61
Moto-Tool 176
MSG Star Trak ball 114
muscle
  action of hand and arm 17
  base of thumb 47
  conscious control 54
  crowding base of thumb 60
  fibers 19
  finger abductor 43
  fingers 43
  relaxed 19
  strengthening 56, 183
  system of forearm 19
  systems of hand 18
  thumb, stretched 60
  toning vs. wrist support 62
  well-balanced 21, 56

N

Nagy, Steve 11, 27, 105
near-in target point 88
New Skin 181
Norris, Joe 185

O

offset thumbhole
  Brunswick 28
  Strickland 28
  using standard centerline 162

P

palm pitch (see adlateral) 42
parallel line bowling .65, 66, 68
PBA Tour 11
perception, awareness 13
perceptive 15

perceptive, becoming 156
Pezzano, Chuck 183
pigment in cover 124
pin
  avoiding bridge contact 62
  deck 143, 151, 155
  design 85
  impact point 98
  reactivity 85
  successful carry 80
pin bowler 75
pitch
  ablateral 43
  adlateral 43
  away (ablateral) 42
  centerline thumbhole 47
  correct fingerhole 46
  defined 39
  forward thumbhole 48
  general considerations 24
  lateral 42
  lateral thumbhole .. 42, 47, 50
  lateral thumbhole vs. turn .. 50
  lateral vs. reverse 50
  measured vs. feel 28
  measuring lateral 50
  middle fingerhole 44
  palm (adlateral) 42
  planes 24, 43
  reverse fingerhole 41
  reverse thumbhole 41, 49
  ring fingerhole 45
  thumbhole 47
  toward (see adlateral) 42
  under (see adlateral) 42
  zero 25, 39
placement distance 68, 69
plane
  alignment 133
  analysis of body position ... 56
  finger tip-to-elbow 17
  fingerholes 162
  forward/reverse thumbhole 30
  forward/reverse thumbhole
    pitch 162

grip centerline 26
long, of arm 57, 60
long, of hand 18
non-circumferential 168
pitch 24, 26, 43, 44
rotating fingerhole pitch ... 162
swing relative to body 130
three-dimensional 40
thumbhole pitch 164
vs. line 40
playing angle
  alignment of body 88
  change to diagonal 86
  compensation factors 94
  components 74
  definition 74
  fine tuning 89
  generalities 76
  inside 81
  in-to-out 83
  outside 78
  straightaway 83
playing lanes (see target line) .. 65
Pliobond (Goodyear) cement 62
porosity of shell 124, 140, 141, 148
power ... 18, 19, 24, 43, 53, 55, 104
Pro Grip rubber inserts 61

R

Randolph Classic Bowling Balls 114
range of motion, base thumb joint 28
Rangefinder 70, 72, 76
rat tail file 179
Ravielli, Anthony 184
relaxation
  defined 21
  hand 19, 20
  importance 20

insecure grip 21
necessary for control 19
total body 19
upper arm vs. forearm 19
release
  clean 35, 47, 48
  faster 50
  leverage 31
reverse fingerhole pitch 41
reverse thumbhole pitch 41
reverse thumbhole pitch vs. lateral pitch 50
reverse thumbhole pitch, recommended 49
ring fingerhole
  direction of flex 46
  pitch 45
roll characteristics 24, 103, 137
rotary sander 37
rotation of thumb at release ..47
Roto Star Bowling Balls 104
round rasp 179
rubbing
  alcohol 125, 180
  compound 124, 176
  on fingers 58

S

Salvino, Carmen 159
sander
  bevel 37, 38
  drum 178, 179
  problem 176, 178
sandpaper 124, 178, 180
Sarge Easter grip 27
Schenkel, Chris 11
Schwoegler, Connie 169
scoring potential ..85, 127, 128, 143, ... 149, 152, 158
scratches on shell 124, 140, 141
self-hypnosis 20, 159, 186

self-image 9, 150, 159
semifingertip grip
   finger depth issue 27
   indeterminate spans 37
   standard 27
Shaklee's Basic H 125
shaping
   considerations 173
   goals 172
   holes 171
   thumbhole 175
shellac 25, 113
shoes
   custom-made 63
   Lind 63
   part of leverage 63
shot
   appropriate 137
   babying 61
   correcting 158
   cross-lane 147
   decent without blocking 85
   finding quickly 138
   finesse 148
   fudging 61
   going to school on 156
   misdirected 76
   pulled 152, 156
   put-up (block) 145
   repeating 70
   soften 148
   useful 137
shoulders
   linked to fingers 57
   narrow 69
   opening 82
   swinging 154
Showers, Norman E. 184
Side Roller Ball 105
side weight
   common 113
   creating positive 104
   negative 107
   neutral 107

positive 107
synthetic lane 156
six-foot level dots 88
size
   bridge 24
   starting holes 24
skid
   decreased V 134
   deep weight center 115
   effect of bottom weight ... 110
   finger/thumb weight 141
   full roller 113
   horizontal rotation 135
   less with earlier roll 136
   minimum V 134
   plastic vs. rubber 141
   shallow weight center 115
   sufficient 143
   vs. oil-soaked lane 152
   vs. roll dynamics 116
   vs. total weight 141
slide
   desirable characteristics 55
   long 55
   pins off of deck 152
   pushing into 92
   vs. flatness of swing 55
Smith, Harry "Tiger" 61
soaker ball 122, 125
soft shot 148
Solomon, J. B. 157
span
   clean release 35
   correctness 35
   defined 23
   direction of 48, 50, 174
   error in fitting 23, 36
   excessive 24, 35, 45
   feel of appropriate 35
   fingertip 45
   fitting 24
   general considerations 23
   insufficient 36
   lines 164
   narrow 37, 51

203

preservation of 172
scale 177
stretching 18
underspanned 24, 36
variance 36
vs. pitch 37
spare
   adjust stance position 99
   center 147
   combinations simplified 98
   corner 147
   shooting 97
spot bowling 67, 75
spraying the shot 76
St. John, Jim 129
stance
   adjust for target line 66
   ensures accuracy 74
   imbalance during 54
   mismatch to target line 76
   modifying position 89, 92
   moving feet 74, 90
   position defined 74
   shift during league session 86
static
   balance 119
   beam balance . 116, 117, 119
static weight
   beam balance readings ... 116
steps
   ball construction 105
   cadence 133
   drift 92
   error in path 93
   path of 74
Strickland offset thumbhole grip
   defined 28
   rationale 28
   steps in drilling 162
   vs. standard grip 167
subconscious
   control 21
   detects tension 21
   effort 55

mind 20
summation of internal forces .56
Super Glue 62
Superior Bowling Club 105
surface properties
   cleanliness 125
   coverstock 121
   hardness 122
   pigment in the shell 124
   porosity 124
   scratches 124
swing
   compensation for aberrant .89
   convergent 91
   divergent 92
   effortless power 55
   error in plane 90
   finesse on blocked lane ...147
   flat 55
   length vs. ball speed 136
   length vs. speed of steps .133
   relative to body plane 130
   security 31
   speed 130
   speed vs. followthrough ...133
   tension vs. oily lane 153
   timing vs. release point 135

T

tangential offset 31
tape
   3M (Scotch) Company 180
   cloth, gripping 180
   Super Tuftex All-Purpose .180
   vinyl, tighten holes 180
target 57
target line
   12-to-10 80
   18-to-15 82
   22-to-18 82
   3-to-3 77
   5-to-5 79
   8-to-8 79
   action of ball on 67

adjusting 86
alignment with bowling arm 76
determining hook size 83
gradual shift 86
modify for aberrant swing .. 89
out-to-in 83
pivoting for spares 99
troubleshooting 84
vs. approach line 68, 76
vs. arrow level point 76
vs. ball path 57
vs. break point 76
vs. drift 93
vs. foul line 57
vs. foul line point 76
vs. stance position 66, 94
vs. target point 76
target point
  near-in 88
  vs. target line 76
targeting system
  developing personal 68
  dot/arrow 67
  elements 67
  logical 65
  Rangefinder 6
Taylor, Bill 49, 50, 53, 104, 107,
  .... 118, 163, 186
Taylor, Dawson 20, 55, 183
tension
  conscious interference 20
  created by unsteady steps . 55
  death grip on ball 18
  minimum desired 19
  misfit of grip 162
  vs. control 19
  vs. fear 21
  vs. oily lane condition 153
Thermosafe 144
three-hole conventional grip . 26
thumb
  90-degrees to fingers 18
  action 47
  base joint 28, 50
  base joint, range of motion 28

beginning hole size 24, 37
bowling glove effect 62
callous formation 48
clean release 133
comfort vs. standard grip ... 58
considerations 174
direction of span 48
drop freely into hole 35
excessive size 37
flexed in fist 17
forward/reverse pitch 49
full insertion while fitting 24
gripping face 48, 175
gripping surface 47
inserts 37
lateral pitch 42
muscle systems 24
offset grip abandoned 32
rotation at release 47
use of air vent 172
varying release position ... 134
vs. excessive span 27
vs. middle finger flexion 30
thumbhole
  bevel 174
  fitting goal 48
  pitch 47
  pitch vs. action of thumb 47
  proper starting size 37
  reverse pitch 49
  tangential offset 31
Tiger Grip inserts 61
timing difficulties 20
too technical 66, 187
tooling 38
top weight
  error 112
  static measurement 112
touchdown point 76, 86
toward pitch (see adlateral) .. 42
track
  ball, closer to fingers 107
  ball, closer to thumb 107
  ball, full roller 112
  ball, loaded axis 117

ball, lowering 50
ball, sanding restriction ... 124
ball, vs. centerline 107
lane, absent on ideal 79
lane, dry (tunnel block) 147
lane, oil migration 139
lane, playing dry 151
lane, railroad imagery 76
lane, wear with play 86
turn
   ball in holding cradle 32
   conventional grip 27
   effect later break point 79
   full roller release 112
   hips, avoid action 82
   retaining potential 27
   rotate fingers on insertion .. 35
   semifingertip grip 27
   strain on finger muscles 43
   thumb rotation at release .. 37
   vs. lateral thumbhole pitch 50
   vs. out-to in target line 83
   when imparted 134
two-finger grip 25

U

under pitch (see adlateral) 42

W

web (see bridge) 23
weight block
   composition 105
   deep 117
   design 114
   position in ball 106
   shallow 117
   shape 104
   shifting 106
weight calculation error 112
weight center
   shift 106
weight center shift
   affects axis 113
   correction 163

defined 106
influence of pitch 163
unplanned 108
Weight Concept Theory (Yetitto)
.... 104
weight distribution
   early work 104
   part of bag of shots 137
   personalities 103
Welu, Billy 11, 27, 66, 187
Williams, Dr. Roger J. 159
Wilman, Joe 185
wrist
   cupped 17, 60
   supports 62
wrist-to-finger tip axis 41

Y

Yetitto, Vincent "Viny" 104
yoga breathing. 159

Z

zero pitch 25, 39

Figures

Figure 1: Movement of the Hand at the Wrist 16

Figure 2: The Muscle Systems of the Hand – The muscle mass of the thumb is roughly ninety degrees to the abductor and adductor muscles of the fingers. 18

Figure 3: The Muscle System of the Forearm Showing Tendons Leading to the Fingers (FT) 21

Figure 4: A Typical Grip Layout Measurement Sheet (Courtesy of Roy "Pete" Moore and Bob Tomlinson) 22

Figure 5: Various Types of Grip 26

Figure 6: In A, the thumbhole is tangent to the centerline; in B, it is superimposed on the centerline. Span M equals span X; span R equals span Y. 29

Figure 7: Label View of Three Different Grips (note clockface reference) 30

Figure 8: View of Three Grips with the Label at the Top (T) 31

Figure 9: The Correct Spans for a Fingertip Grip 36

Figure 10: .Different Perspectives of a Bowling Ball Using a Clockface Reference System 40

Figure 11: Reverse pitch (R) is the opposite of forward pitch (F). The directions of reference for thumb and finger forward/reverse pitch are 180 degrees different. 41

Figure 12: Reference Points of Pitch 42

Figure 13: Pitch Terminology for a Right-handed Grip – A. Directions of forward (F) and reverse (R) pitch. B. Directions or right lateral (RL) and left lateral (LL) pitch. 42

207

Figure 14: Lateral Pitch Terminology
LL= left lateral, RL = right lateral, AB = ablateral, AD = adiateral.. 43

Figure 15:
A. The direction of flex (DF) of the middle finger is parallel with the grip layout centerline (CL).
B. Label View: On the surface of the ball, the centers of the middle fingerhole and the thumbhole lie on the same line (MT).
C. Bottom View: The angle of pitch of the middle fingerhole should be parallel with the centerline plane.
D. 6 O'Clock View: Showing parallelism of MH and CL planes
E. 6 O'Clock View: The thumbhole pitch plane (TH) intersects plane CL... 44

Figure 16: Ring Fingerhole Pitch – The direction of flex of the ring finger (DF) is not usually parallel with the grip layout centerline plane (CL). It may intersect this plane because of individual hand characteristics and because of the conformity of the hand to the ball surface (ARC)... 45

Figure 17: Options of Pitch Based Upon a Different Starting Position For the Top of the Thumbhole – In both cases A and B, the thumbhole axis would pass through the geometric center of the ball if zero pitch were chosen. 46

Figure 18: A Comparison of the Directions of Flex of the Fingers and Thumb (DF) and the Direction of the Span (DS) 48

Figure 19: A Plane Analysis of the Body Position at the Foul Line 56

Figure 20: Alignment of the Grip Layout Centerline (CL) with the Long Plane of the Arm (P4) in the Offset Thumbhole Grip (A) and in the Standard Grip (B) 59

Figure 21: A Cutdown Version of the Bowling Lane and Approach – Note how the pins align with the dots and arrows of the Rangefinder system. The numbers indicate the board width distance away from the right and left channels. The "X" denotes the 17th (strike pocket) board 72

Figure 22: A Roughly-scaled Diagram of the Lane and Approach – Note the proportional relationships among the lengths of the sections 73

Figure 23: Three Outside Playing Angles
A. A 3-to-3 target line
B. A 5-to-5 target line
C. An 8-to-8 target line 78

Figure 24: Three Inside Playing Angles
A. A 12-to-10 target line
B. A 18-to-15 target line
C. A 22-to-18 target line 81

Figure 25: Adjusting the Target Line Around a Foul Line (B) and Around an Arrow-level (C) Pivot Point 87

Figure 26: Modifying the Stance Position to Compensate for a Divergent Swing 89

Figure 27: Modifying the Stance Position to Compensate for a Convergent Swing 91

Figure 28: Steps in The Manufacture of a Bowling Ball – The core (C) is made first, the weight block (W) is added, then the shell (S) is molded around them. The punch mark (PM) indicates the position of the weight center, and the label is engraved around the punch mark 106

Figure 29: Influence of Placement of the Weight Center on the Roll of a Semiroliing Ball 107

Figure 30: Movement of the Weight Center After Drilling a Fingertip Grip Around the Punch Mark (PM) – ThIs is the incidental "hole size weight shift." The weight center moves in the direction where less material is removed. 109

Figure 31: A Comparison of the Fingertip Grip (A) With the Conventional Grip (B) with Respect to the Amount of Weight Removed by Drilling the Holes—The fractions denote the hole diameter in inches. 109

209

Figure 32: Positioning of the Center of Bottom Weight (BW) Relative to a Right-Handed Grip to Achieve Lateral Weight (A) and Finger/Thumb Weight (B) 111

Figure 33: A Comparison of the Full Roller Track (A) and the Semiroller Track (B) With Respect to Weight Placement and Axis of Rotation (AR)................. 113

Figure 34: Various Weight Block Designs – The stripes indicate material that is denser than the rest of the ball. Diagram H does not show a true weight block. All perspectives are the same as in diagram A. 114

Figure 35: A Comparison of Deep and Shallow Weight Centers (W) – The deep weight center is closer to the geometric center of the ball than to the surface. The opposite Is true for the shallow weight center 115

Figure 36: Assigning Arbitrary Distances Between the Ball Center and the Deep (Z1) and Shallow (Z2) Weight Centers — In both cases, the top weight is two ounces. 116

Figure 37: A Typical Beam (Static) Balance and a Ball Showing the Axes of Measured Finger/Thumb and Lateral Weights (C is the center of the grip) 118

Figure 38: The Process of Increasing Adaptive Range (collecting a bag of shots).................. 131

Figure 39: Variable Hand Positions 135

Figure 40: The Bowling Lane at the Level of the Arrows – The numbers indicate the board in which the arrow is imbedded (counting from the channel inward). EO = extreme outside line, O = outside line, I = inside line, and EI = extreme inside line 142

Figure 41: Four Common lane Conditions.................. 144

Figure 42: Three Additional Lane Conditions – The last diagram shows a sequence of playing angles. 153

Figure 43: A. The grip layout centerline (CL) is drawn slightly to the right of the offset thumbhole grip center (G3). For a right-handed grip, G3 should be located as shown if finger weight and side weight are desired. (L = the label) B. Span Lines (SL) and bridge lines (BL) are added. C. The thumbhole pitch plane reference line (MT) is drawn. D. The ring fingerhole span line lies on an arc (R) drawn with the near edge of the thumbhole as the pivot point. 164

Figure 44: A Comparison of a Standard Grip (A), a Strickland Offset Thumbhole Grip (B), and the Brunswick Standard Offset Grip (C) 167

Figure 45: A Graph Showing a Comparison of Weight Removal Figures from Three Different Sources – The figures shown are for a 2-1/2 inch deep hole. 170

Figure 46: A Bowling Ball with Lines Representing the Directions of Spans Between Thumb and Finger Holes 173

Figure 47: A Closer Look at the Fingerholes of the Ball Shown in Figure 46, b = the bridge... 173

Figure 48: A Closer Look at the Thumbhole of the Ball Shown in Figure 46. 174

Figure 49: A. Bevel Terminology: L = light, M = moderate, H = heavy, VH = very heavy. B. Improper Bevel Types: The angle of the bevel is other than 45 degrees to the surface of the ball. C. Improper Shaping of the Hole: 1. the cone-shaped hole, 2. the urn-shaped hole, 3. and 4. irregularly-shaped holes... 176

Figure 50: Recommended Tools for the Beveling and Shaping of the Holes in a Bowling Ball) 177

Tables

Table 1: Compensation Factors for Two Bowlers Using the Same Six Playing Angles 94

Table 2: Board Numbers of Desired Spare Destinations at the Pins 98

Table 3: A Review of the Variable Characteristics of a Bowling Ball – The spans and hole sizes as well as the size of the ball are not variable. 140

Table 4: Effects of Changing Certain Variables on the Action of the Ball on an Ideal Lane Condition. 140

Table 5: The Amount of Weight Removed by the Drilling of Various Hole Sizes – For a comparison of these numbers with those of Bill Taylor and of the AMF Company, see Figure 45. These numbers are well within the limits of accuracy of the beam balance................. 168

Table 6: Distance of Shift of the Weight Center Due to Pitch – The center of the weight moves in the direction of pitch. 169

Table 7: Pitch and Bridge Requirements of Some of the Brunswick Patented Grips – Pitches that measure true are marked with an asterisk (*). Ad = adlateral (away from the thumb side of the hand), Ab = ablateral (toward the thumb side of the hand), Lat. = lateral. .. 169

www.ingramcontent.com/pod-product-compliance
Lightning Source LLC
Chambersburg PA
CBHW070646160426
43194CB00009B/1603